The Ultimate
CHEAPSKATE'S
ROAD MAP TO TRUE RICHES

The Ultimate
CHEAPSKATE'S
ROAD MAP TO TRUE RICHES

A Practical (and Fun) Guide to Enjoying
Life More by Spending Less

JEFF YEAGER

Broadway Books
New York

BROADWAY

PUBLISHED BY BROADWAY BOOKS

Published in the United States by Broadway Books, an imprint of The
Doubleday Broadway Publishing Group, a division of Random House, Inc.,
New York.
www.broadwaybooks.com

BROADWAY BOOKS and its logo, a letter B bisected on the diagonal, are
trademarks of Random House, Inc.

The following book is nonfiction. That is, with the exception of those
characters, passages, people, events, dialogue, and other stuff that I made up,
embellished, or, at the age of fourteen, once fantasized about in the privacy of
the family bathroom. Furthermore, I composed approximately every eleventh
page of this book following one of my infamous Box Wine Happy Hours.
Imagine a group of like-minded cheapskates, passing around an $11.95 five-
liter box of Peter Vella's Chablis (which I'm told is French for "in a box"),
drinking from the plastic spigot like so many happy hummingbirds. So
obviously I can't be held accountable for those sections of this book either.

Like all books about personal finance, this book is intended as a general
guide. You should seek the advice of a qualified personal finance professional
about your individual financial situation and plans. That person will
undoubtedly issue a similar disclaimer about the advice they give you, but that
disclaimer will cost a lot more than the $12.95 you paid for this book. (Having
said all that, I hardly think that the basic advice offered in this book—"Spend
less money, for chrissake!"—will cause harm or injury to anyone.)

And finally, a word of warning for truly hardcore cheapskates: Should
reading this book result in an erection lasting four hours or longer, you're
obviously one sick skinflint and should seek immediate medical attention.
Remember, "It's only money, so who needs it?"

Library of Congress Cataloging-in-Publication Data
Yeager, Jeff.
    The Ultimate cheapskate's road map to true riches: a practical (and fun)
guide to enjoying life more by spending less / by Jeff Yeager.—1st ed.
       p.   cm.
    1. Finance, Personal. I. Title

HG179. Y43 2008
332.024—dc22   2007034883

ISBN 978-0-7679-2695-9

PRINTED IN THE UNITED STATES OF AMERICA

10 9 8 7 6 5 4 3 2 1

First Edition

To Denise, my pooooor wife

CONTENTS

ACKNOWLEDGMENTS

Saying thank you is a prime example of what this book is all about, something of tremendous value and importance that costs absolutely nothing.

And since publishers traditionally allocate an entire page or two for that purpose—whether the author writes six words or six hundred—you can bet I'll maximize the return on my non-investment.

First, for those most immediately responsible for making me the Ultimate Cheapskate: Jim Bell, Margaret Pergler, Betsy Alexander, Rainy Farrell, and NBC's *Today* show for giving me my cheap shot; Stacey Glick and Dystel & Goderich Literary Management for taking on America's cheapest man as their cheapest client; Dan Zak at the *Washington Post* for writing about me when it counted most; Kelly Knight, Mark Stevens, and Steve Medley at WARW's *Stevens & Medley Morning Show* for generously sharing their airtime; and Gary Foreman at www.Stretcher.com for publishing the best frugal stuff on the Internet, including some of mine. And, of course, Michelle Singletary of the *Washington Post*, for both rejecting and accepting me—the story of my life, sort of—and the excellent financial advice she provides her readers each week in her nationally syndicated column, "The Color of Money."

I'm forever indebted to the good folks at Broadway Books for publishing this book, such as it is. Most of all I'm beholden to Kristine Puopolo, my omni-excellent editor, for continually reminding me to make it funnier (silly me, I forgot) and teaching me about the proper use of exclamation marks!!!

And to my loyal Miser Advisers and other supporters, many of whom will see themselves (perhaps disguised) in these pages, including Eugene Balaguer, the Bookbinder family, Jerry Dyson, Grace Griffith, Nancy Heisel, Michelle Hillman, Dave Kalter, Tim Kelly, Doug Maas, Denise Owen, Belinda Rollins, Kathy Schmiesing, Marta Tellado, and my Miser Adviser Emeritus, Ralph Huber, for his friendship when the going was rough and for his good humor throughout.

So many people are responsible for my education and career in the nonprofit world, the backbone of this book, including the Three Wise Men of Hostelling International USA: Bill Nelson for his lessons in leadership and storytelling, Bob Beard for his longtime friendship and support, and the late Robert B. Johnson Jr., who taught me a lifetime of lessons about life and nonprofit management during his own too short years.

Most of all, I thank my family: my grandparents, Ellen and Clyde Yeager and Irma and Tex Cooper, for giving me so many of the memories and stories you'll hear shortly; my parents, Joyce and Doug, for giving me life and showing me how to truly enjoy it; and my brother, Joel, for all the good times growing up and all the good times to come (you just know we were born to be crusty old men together).

Above all else, I want to thank Denise, my pooooor wife, for always loving and believing in me, even when I was neither lovable nor believable.

One of the greatest luxuries of breaking free of the shekel shackles, as you'll learn how to do in the pages ahead, is that you'll no longer need to associate with anyone you don't like. In writing this book, I had the free joy of interacting not just with people I really like but only with people I really love.

PREFACE: Who Is the Ultimate Cheapskate?

It's true. I'm cheap, and I'm a loser.

In fact the *best* thing that's happened to me over the past few years—the highlight of my ostensibly lowlife existence—is that I entered the 2005 Penny Pincher of the Year Contest sponsored by national finance columnist Michelle Singletary, and—you guessed it—I lost.

Me, the Titan of Tightwads, the Maestro of Misers, the Commander in Cheap. Not only did Singletary shaft me for the fifty-dollar top prize, but I didn't even get an honorable mention in the long list of my cheapskate brethren whose names and frugal tips appeared in her column.

I was crushed. I'd been eyeing a reduced-for-quick-sale rump roast and other ripening delicacies at my local supermarket for a week. I'd all but spent that fifty bucks.

I lost all interest in things that I once found enjoyable. Like double-coupon days and checking the coin return at every public pay phone I pass. I was a broken shell of a miser (although BTW, if you find a broken egg in a carton at the store, it'll usually give you the whole dozen for free).

Denise, my wife of twenty-two years, became concerned. It was as if my frugal libido had gone limp, as limp as the half-priced asparagus I once gleefully loaded into our shopping cart. Her jaw dropped in disbelief one day when I pulled into the closest gas station to fill up without even circling the block to check the prices of the competition.

"Jeff, this has to stop," she said with equal parts concern and mocking disdain in her voice. *"I know I married the cheapest man in America.* What does Michelle Singletary know? She's not married to you, is she?" I detected a distinct wishful inflection in the tone of Denise's last rhetorical question.

It's often occurred to me that most good things in my life have happened when I'm wearing only underwear.

Two weeks after learning of my defeat in the *Post*'s contest, I was sitting in my underwear one Wednesday morning opening a spamish-sounding e-mail from TODAYshow.com. I should explain that I frequently work in only my underwear, particularly since I concluded my twenty-five-year career as an executive in the nonprofit sector and became, as I like to say, *selfishly employed* as a freelance writer.

"You don't know me," the message began, "but first let me say that I think you should have won the $50." The message immediately had my undivided attention.

The producer went on to explain that the *Today* show was starting a new weeklong "Cheapskate Way" series. Michelle Singletary was going to be a guest, and Singletary had been asked if she knew of anyone who had a lighthearted take on the subject matter. She passed along my (losing) contest entry to the *Today* show folks, and within a week I was chatting it up on live TV with Matt Lauer, who aptly branded me the Ultimate Cheapskate and restored my flagging faith in my own frugality.

And so I owe my gig as a guest correspondent on the *Today* show and my blossoming new career as a writer to my two greatest virtues: I'm cheap, and I'm a loser.

Now, I'm flattered when people think I'm funny. Not only is laughter the best medicine, but it's the only one drug companies aren't ripping us off for.

But the fact is, I actually believe what I say and practice what I preach. Well, at least the parts that aren't BS. But I'm sure you'll be able to recognize those.

OK, so to save time and energy costs, I sometimes soft-boil my morning eggs along with the dirty dishes in the dishwasher (top shelf for runny yolks, bottom shelf for firm), but who doesn't? (True.)

Some cheapskates save the wrapping paper off their Christmas gifts to use again next year. Not me. I save it, put it back on the roll, and return it to Wal-Mart for a refund. Gotcha. That's BS (although it might not be a bad act of civil disobedience when the last woodlot in your neighborhood is torn down to put up another Wal-Mart).

And I *re-cant*, as opposed to *decant*, the wine I proudly serve to my dinner guests, funneling cheap box wine into premium-label bottles I've collected over the years. And you know what? No one has *ever* questioned the authenticity of the wines I've served, which proves either there's no difference in taste or wine snobs live in fear of being exposed as frauds, not daring to question the label on the bottle. (True.)

And I never buy postage stamps. Instead I practice a technique I call "reverse mailing." I address an envelope to myself, put the intended recipient as the return address, and drop it in a mail box without a stamp. The post office kindly "returns" it to the intended recipient marked "Postage Due." (False.) Nah, I don't do that. It would be wrong. I imagine it's also illegal, and

I've always heard that prison inmates go extra hard on philatelists doing time in the big house.

The truth is, I'm forty-eight years old at the time I'm writing this, and I believe that even in my relatively short lifetime we've seen a fundamental—and fundamentally *bad*—shift in our values and priorities.

We are now a people and a nation focused more on amassing a quantity of stuff than we are on amassing a quality of life. Making money is no longer a means to an end; it's an end in itself. Somewhere along the line this shift of values and priorities happened. It happened to our country, it happened to our generation, and I'll bet it happened to you.

If money, and the stuff you can buy with it, have become your dominatrix, if you remember your kids' ages by which model of cell phone you were using at the hospital when they were born, then I think this book might help.

This book is about two things: getting more for less and, even more important, understanding that less *is* often more. It's about the fact that you probably already have everything you could ever need or want, if you'll only slow down long enough on the Road to Riches to think about it.

What I Really Believe

Living on less is a good thing to do. It's the only financial advice that will work for almost everyone. It's about a quality of life you cannot buy, a sense of satisfaction you cannot fake, and an appreciation for others that gives life value. It's also about helping save the planet and sharing with those in need. Living on less can be funny, but it's not a joke.

—Jeff Yeager
The Ultimate Cheapskate
UltimateCheapskate.com

1

Introduction: The Money Step

I always stay at the cheapest hotel, so I was surprised to find a mint on my pillow in the evening. Turns out it fell out of the mouth of the guy who slept there the night before. —Jeff Yeager, the Ultimate Cheapskate

Rule No. 1: Groceries do not count as Christmas gifts, even if you gift wrap them. —Denise Yeager, pooooor wife of the Ultimate Cheapskate, giving Jeff the annual holiday gift buying lecture.

Man, money may not be the root of all evil, but it's a seed that can sprout some pretty nasty shit. —anonymous barroom philosopher I met in The Bar, Williston, North Dakota, summer 1977, while I was on a cross-country bicycle trip. He was bemoaning the recent breakup with his "old lady," a rift that grew out of the couple's winning one thousand dollars in the lottery.

What's your earliest childhood memory of money?

Close your eyes and think about it hard for a minute, because it's really important. The memory you eventually dredge up may have a shockingly familiar feeling. In fact you may conjure up feelings and emotions that crossed the radar screen of your mind this very day, as you paid for your groceries, wrote a check to the electric company, or shelled out the kid's weekly allowance.

Keep that memory at the very top of your mind as we travel in the pages ahead down some of life's major byways, byways filled with intersections, with choices. Not just choices about money and how to spend it, but decisions about what you want out of life, what's important in life, and what money does—or doesn't—have to do with any of it.

I'll bet that your earliest thoughts and memories of money are still influencing some of the financial decisions you make today. As you keep barreling down the Road to Riches, convinced, as most of us are, that the intersection with the Highway to Happiness is just around the next bend, it's worth spending a moment to think about how you got to this point. Like consulting a road map when you're already hopelessly lost, you might be surprised to find out where you really are and that the course you are on is leading you away from your intended destination.

In my case, my earliest memory of money is, ironically, of found money, of a shiny silver dime, probably dated around 1963, when I was five. I found it while playing in our front yard on Summerfield Road in Sylvania, Ohio.

In my case, my first taste of money truly was a *taste*. By the time my mom sprinted across the yard to see what I was playing with, it was too late. I had already swallowed it. In addition to the spellbinding shine of the coin, I remember the metallic flavor as it traveled awkwardly down my tiny throat. Somehow, through the marvels of the human body and mind, I still get a slight, almost undetectable taste of metal in my mouth at the end of every day when I empty out my pocket change.

Money on the Brain

Like it or not, money is part of our very being. We worry more about money than anything else. We fight with our spouses and families more about money than anything else. We spend more of our waking hours earning and spending money than doing anything else.

In fact I read about a research study a few years ago that showed that people think about money an average of fifty-five times a day. That immediately caught my attention, as I also remembered reading about another study that showed that people (or, rather, men) think about sex an average of every fifteen minutes throughout the day.

When you combine the results of these two studies and subtract out of a twenty-four-hour period the number of hours spent sleeping and the hours spent thinking about nothing at all, if I've done the math correctly, you discover something startling. Not only do most people think _only_ about money and sex, but a good deal of the time men are thinking about money and sex simultaneously. On second thought, I guess I don't find it that surprising.

So with thoughts of money dominating your every waking hour and encroaching on every aspect of your life, you pick up a book about—what else?—money.

But unlike most personal finance books, this book is not about how to make _more_ money. This book is about how to make _less_ money, but how to be happier than if you made more. It's about how to make money less a part of your life by spending less, so that you can enjoy life more. And it's not so much about finding the best values in things—although it provides some good advice in that regard—as about valuing the best things, which usually come without price tags.

Most of all, this book is about *choices*, not about sacrifices, as my moniker, the Ultimate Cheapskate, might make you think. It's about the choices we make every day about earning and spending money and the priorities we set for ourselves on the basis of those choices.

The Money Step

Ultimately each of the choices we're going to look at in this book—whether it's what kind of house you should buy or whether you have enough roughage in your diet—is a choice involving the Money Step.

The Money Step is the little dance of earning and spending we do pretty much every day of our life. It has three beats, like a waltz:

> **Earning money**
> **To spend money**
> **To get what you want**
> **[. . . or at least what you think you want]**

The Money Step has become the default setting for the world we live in today. It's now the rule, not the exception. We unconsciously, or consciously, take the Money Step when doing almost everything we do. The idea of getting what we *really* want by reducing or even entirely skipping the Money Step— a comfortable house without an uncomfortable mortgage, strong health without ever buying a gym membership, the ability to sleep nights knowing that we're debt free—is a concept so out of vogue in our society it's nearly extinct.

As we'll see, questioning the Money Step is as much about deciding what you truly want and need as about deciding how best to get it. By the end of this book I hope you'll start to question whether the Money Step should continue to be the default setting in your life. And throughout this book, as we look at different big-ticket items in the typical family budget, I encourage you to keep one key question in mind: Can you and your family skip, or at least limit, the Money Step and go straight to the real prize?

The Allegory of the Ax and the Basketball

I first came to appreciate—indeed fixate on—the Money Step during my twenty-five-year career as a CEO and fundraiser in the nonprofit sector. Operating in an environment where money is always scarce and goals are rarely measured just in dollars, I spent my days finding creative ways to avoid, or at least mitigate as much possible, the Money Steps that stood between my organization and the mission it was created to serve.

You might say that my vocation as a nonprofit manager was achieving success without the use of money, or at least without a lot of it. "The nonprofit sector is fortunate to be immune from economic downturns," I used to tell my staff, "because in the nonprofit world, the economy always sucks." Much of what I learned during those years rubbed off on my personal life and finances, or maybe the other way around, making my transition to the Ultimate Cheapskate a natural one.

But looking back on it now, I guess I should have grasped the concept of the Money Step years before, as a result of a horrifically embarrassing incident in my youth. The symbolic significance of the episode was lost on me at the time, but I now understand and deeply appreciate the prophetic importance of what I call the Allegory of the Ax and the Basketball.

When I was at the age of sixteen, an age not associated with great wisdom, yet one at which you've presumably learned something about the basic laws of physics, my brother, Joel, and I were chopping firewood along the banks of the Maumee River in rural Ohio. The winter ice had just broken, and with the spring melt the water was running high. The driftwood was piling up along the shoreline faster than we could cut and split it.

If you've never witnessed an ice breakup on a river of any size, I can tell you it's a powerful event. Foot-thick chunks of ice churned down the riverbed, sounding like a crushed ice dispenser on the door of an expensive refrigerator. The ice flows packed so much speed and power that occasionally they'd pitch a live catfish or sucker out of the water and onto the shore. You couldn't live on a riverbank as we did and not mark the year by the day the ice breaks.

When the ice breaks up, it pushes anything and everything downstream—not just driftwood but flotsam and jetsam of all kinds. Growing up, we'd seen it all: pontoon boats, beer kegs, duck blinds, ice chests, furniture, oil drums, refrigerators, a travel trailer, and our most prized recovery, a store mannequin with lifelike breasts (or at least we thought so at that age). This particular day the pickings were a little slim, but a plump basketball eventually came along, just close enough to the shore that we could wade into the icy water and pull it in with a long stick.

Although my brother and I both are well over six feet tall, we are Yeagers and thus far too uncoordinated to actually play basketball. We had little use for the newfound treasure, despite the peril involved in rescuing it. We took turns hurling the ball at each other, bouncing it off some rocks and trees, and we'd all but lost interest in it when my brother had a proposition for me.

"Hey, Gook [his brotherly term of endearment for me], I'll give you five bucks if you can chop it in half with the ax," he said, pointing at the basketball. To reinforce his point, he produced a soggy five-dollar bill from the pocket of his blue jeans.

"What is he, crazy?" I thought. "Easy money!"

Without a second thought, I picked up the ax, swung it high above my head, and brought it down on the basketball with all my heft. I wasn't just going to chop it in half; I was going to obliterate that thing.

Frankly, it *never*—even for a nanosecond—occurred to me that the basketball might withstand the blow of the ax. All I was thinking about at the time was what I would do with the money and how good I'd feel pulling the five-spot out of my brother's hand. I was so focused on the money that the possible consequences of the endeavor never crossed my mind.

Gosh, telling the story now, I feel so stupid. Of course the ax didn't puncture the basketball, and since I'd swung it with such passion, the force of the ricochet redoubled off the taut ball. The ax rebounded instantaneously, the flat back hitting me squarely in the forehead, right between the eyes.

I staggered backward, my lanky teenage frame reeling. My vision blurred as if I were suddenly inside the lava lamp in my bedroom, looking out. The last thing I remember before I passed out and fell to the ground was the sight of my brother falling to the ground first, bent double in a fit of uncontrollable laughter.

After I came to—well, actually, about thirty years after I came to—I realized three important things about this spectacularly stupid incident:

1. I assumed that getting the money would be easy.
2. The possible consequences of trying to get the money never crossed my mind.
3. Because of No. 1 and No. 2, it never occurred to me

that maybe I shouldn't try to get the money, that I
should skip the Money Step.

Does any of that sound familiar? Maybe it even hits *you* right
between the eyes?

But where does that leave us as we lead our lives in this era
of abundance, with unlimited opportunities to chase after more
money and a perennial search for genuine happiness? If more
money and more stuff aren't the key to happiness, is it possible,
as I learned when I brought that ax down on the basketball,
that their pursuit might actually lead us to greater *un*happiness?

Money: It's Not All It's Cracked Up to Be

If money talks, then it tells a lot of lies. That's not just the conclusion I've come to in my own life, the reason I've decided to
embrace rather than *shun* my Inner Miser, but it's a conclusion
supported by the experience of an increasing number of the su-
perrich, like Bill Gates and Warren Buffett, as they strive to rid
themselves of at least some of their wealth. Talking about his
ranking as the world's richest man, Gates said, "I wish I wasn't.
There is nothing good that comes of that."

Researchers who study such things report that when it comes
to the relationship between wealth and happiness, there's not
much to report. There really isn't one. Daniel Gilbert, a professor of psychology at Harvard, writes in his thought-provoking
book *Stumbling on Happiness* (Alfred A. Knopf, 2006):

> Economists and psychologists have spent decades study-
> ing the relation between wealth and happiness, and they
> have generally concluded that wealth increases human

happiness when it lifts people out of abject poverty and into the middle class but that it does little to increase happiness thereafter. . . . It hurts to be hungry, cold, sick, tired, and scared, but once you've bought your way out of these burdens, the rest of your money is an increasingly useless pile of paper.

My experience as a professional fundraiser dealing with some extremely wealthy people convinced me that Gilbert and other social scientists speak the truth: There is no relationship between wealth and happiness beyond some point just north of the U.S. poverty line. In the nonprofit sector, perhaps more than in any other area, you get a chance to interact with both extremes of the economic spectrum, very wealthy donors and very needy clients. Even though it's a purely anecdotal observation, I can tell you that the multimillionaires I've met have generally struck me as less joyful than lots of folks I've encountered on the other end of the teeter-totter and as usually much less content than most of us in between. I think Ben Franklin nailed it: "Who is rich? He that rejoices in his portion."

Enough *Is* Enough

How much money do you want? That's the question I asked time after time as I spoke with people while writing this book. That's the question I want you to ask yourself right now. Forget about whether it's an attainable amount or a rational goal, and answer it as you would a word association test, with the first thing that pops into your mind. (If you're a guy, I know that it's hard to see past the naked ladies dancing on the stage of your frontal lobe, but go ahead and try.)

If you're like most people I've spoken to, you may not have an answer, or at least a *real answer*—that is, an answer that's objective, precise, or even quantifiable. Typical responses include:

- "More money than I have now"
- "As much money as I can get"
- "Enough money that I'll never have to worry ever again [*about money, I guess*]"
- "More money than I could ever possibly need"
- No. 1 answer: "More than my &%$# neighbor/brother/sister/father/mother/boss/ex-wife/coworker/etc. has or will ever have!"

Besides lacking specificity, of course the other thing that all these nonanswers have in common is that: whatever the real answer may be, I ain't there yet! I want MORE! As Daniel Gilbert writes, "Once we've eaten our fill of pancakes, more pancakes are not rewarding, hence we stop trying to procure and consume them. But not so, it seems, with money."

Someone once described (well, *blasted*, really) my philosophy of cheapskateism as "settling for less." I initially bristled at that demeaning phrase, protesting that "less can really be more" and that you need not sacrifice your dreams and desires if you're a frugal-meister like me.

But the more I thought about it, the more I came to appreciate both the wisdom and the beauty of the phrase "settling for less."

If the alternative is leading a life that's *unsettled,* a life of always wanting more, then settling for less is a pretty darn good deal. Money is relative—what's a lot of money for one person is very little to someone else, and the other way around—so it's not a matter of a lot or a little, of more or less, but it's all about *enough.*

No Such Thing as a Free Lunch

A few years ago I was having lunch with a longtime friend of mine. Clay F. is close to ten years my senior. While I spent my career toiling away at relatively modest paying jobs in the non-profit sector, Clay unleashed his entrepreneurial zeal in the tech field, starting his first company while he was still in college.

Despite the fact that I could never understand exactly what any of Clay's companies did or produced—something about cold fusion computer technology, which I swear was a rock band I saw in concert at the Toledo Sports Arena in 1973—it's clear that *he* understands it enough for it to make him a very wealthy man.

In fact Clay is about the only friend I have who doesn't try to BOGOF me when the lunch check arrives. If you're not familiar with the term, "BOGOF" refers to "buy one and get one free" (aka "two-for-one-deals" or "twofers"), and in hardened cheapskate circles like mine it's sport to one-up your dining companion by whipping out a two-for-one coupon when the check arrives to pay for your portion of the bill. After all, if the other guy was prepared to pay for his lunch anyway, why shouldn't you be the one to eat for free? As we like to say, in our crowd "no one ever tries to *Bogart* the check, but everyone tries to BOGOF the check." Except for Clay F., that is.

Clay is, without a doubt, one of the most savvy, sophisticated businessmen I know. That's why our conversation over lunch surprised me so. After we caught each other up on family affairs and he tried yet again to explain to me that Java script has nothing to do with either coffee or the fat dude in *Star Wars,* Clay said he was thinking about selling his latest enterprise and retiring. "I just don't know how much money I need before I retire," he said.

That stunned me. Here was a brilliant, accomplished financier, apparently unable to master any of the myriad of retirement savings calculators that pop up and vibrate on my computer screen every time I go online. Maybe Clay wasn't such a computer wiz after all? In fact, I'm sure I still have a Cold Fusion T-shirt from that concert. Could the *F* in Clay F. stand for "faker"?

"What? You know there are a million books on the subject, not to mention all the info available on the Internet. You do know about the Internet, don't you?" I said, baiting him.

"Yeah, yeah. It's not that. Hell, I had more than I could ever *need* by the time I graduated from college and sold my first business. It's more a question of how much I *want*, you know, and when I feel I can, well, *stop*." Clay was unusually serious, as evidenced by his not taking my bait, and I could tell he'd been thinking a lot about this.

"It's funny that you brought this up. I've been thinking about the same thing, sort of. Of course I'm not a techno-geek-gazillionaire like you, but I've always been frugal—"

"Cheap!" He chimed in while I continued speaking.

"—and I've managed to squirrel away a pretty nice nest egg, given my line of work. What I've been thinking about isn't really retirement. I don't know that I ever want to totally retire. I just sort of want to do my own thing, whatever that is on any given day. Kind of, well, afford myself the luxury of being self-employed; or better yet, selfishly employed!" I said.

"Yeager, you missed your calling. You could be writing jingles for toilet bowl cleaners right now. Maybe that's what you should do, once you're *selfishly employed*," he gibed.

"Maybe I will," I said as Clay picked up the check, and I smoothly slid my two-for-one coupon back in my pocket to use another day and scooped the complimentary thin mints off the American Express cashier's tray for my afternoon snack.

Slaying Your *Enoughasaurus*

When do you have *enough*? When can you declare victory in your own personal War for More and call home the troops? The conversation with Clay kept nagging at me, and eventually I had a series of minor epiphanies because of it.

What I came to realize was that despite the vast differences in our net worths, both Clay and I—and everyone else, for that matter—face the same financial challenge: deciding what "enough" is, for you, or slaying your own *Enoughasaurus*.

More is a moving target, not an answer, and leads to the prospect that you'll die in harness, destination unknown. And things like retirement savings calculators can't answer the question for you; they can only help you do the math once you've answered the real question for yourself.

But with a sense of relief, the most important thing I came to realize was that I already had, in spades, the one weapon that is kryptonite to any *Enoughasaurus*. Because I actually enjoy stretching dollars until Washington weeps, I can be happy—indeed happier—with relatively less than I would be with relatively more.

I realized that because of this skill, because of this frugal philosophy, I already had enough. Maybe not enough to retire fully, but enough to quit my full-time job and become selfishly employed, free to pursue my interests and passions without inordinate worry over collecting a regular paycheck. I realized that for a cheapskate like me, it's less about how much I have and more about how much I don't need or don't want. With that, my *Enoughasaurus* gasped its last breath.

Conditioning yourself to spend less and to be content doing so is the way to slay your *Enoughasaurus* too. It's the only financial advice that will work for almost everyone—at least those of us fortunate enough to be above the point of abject poverty. But what may surprise you most in the pages ahead is that a money-"lite" existence is a life of incredible wealth and riches, just not one that involves lots of money.

Grab Your Road Map and Let's Go

Don't be afraid. The cheapskate life that awaits you is anything but grim, dull, or greedy; in fact it's just the opposite.

We'll officially start our journey in the next chapter, after a couple of exercises and thoughts designed to call out your *Enoughasaurus*. In Chapter 2 I'll show you how to go on a fiscal fast, a sort of spending detox, and then I'll share my golden rules for breaking free of the shekel shackles so that we can really get on down the Road to True Riches.

Each of the following chapters (Chapters 3–8) deal with one of life's mega-expenses: food / health, housing, transportation, technology, and entertainment. And even though this is a book about spending less, *not* about making more, Chapter 9 is a bonus chapter on investing (we're not even charging you for Chapter 9), including a glimpse inside the Ultimate Cheapskate's vault. Since to the chagrin of my editor I occasionally lapse into cheapskate vernacular in the pages ahead, following the last chapter you'll find a handy Cheap-Speak Glossary if you need any definitions.

One final note: Unlike most personal finance regimens that must be carefully followed from Step A to Step Zzzzzz in order to be effective, my cheapskate program is like a Chinese menu. Feel free to pick and choose; read a little here and a little there if you like. Follow even one of my prescriptions for purposeful prosperity, and you'll come out ahead—and I bet you'll come back for more.

So put away your wallet—the Road to True Riches is a free-way—and let's go.

✎ EXERCISE: 20 Questions with Gramps

For generations Americans have been concerned about keeping up with the Joneses. But our generation might want to think for a minute about keeping up with their Grandpa Jones.

During the Depression almost 30 percent of our grandparents had no jobs, and another third were employed less than full-time. More than half of all American families were classified as "living below a minimum subsistence level." Annual per capita farm family income *(in today's dollars)* was less than three thousand dollars.

Thankfully today fewer than one in twenty-five of us is unemployed, and our per capita income is more than twenty-two thousand dollars, one of the highest in the world, in all human history. It's hard for us to imagine what it would have been like to live through the Depression, hard to fathom how far we've come and how much better off we are today. In inflation-adjusted dollars, we are today, on average, four and a half times richer than our great-grandparents at the turn of the century.

But today, for the first time since the Depression, we have a negative saving rate. That means we not only spend all our disposable income (i.e., the amount left after we pay taxes) but we also dip into our previous savings and / or borrow money in order to finance our spending sprees.

During the Depression our grandparents spent more than they made in an attempt to avoid inconveniences like starvation and homelessness. But what excuse do we—the most moneyed generation in American history versus the least—have, and does our unprecedented spending really translate into a superior quality of life?

Take a few minutes to play twenty questions with your grandparents, and draw your own conclusions about whether you're keeping up with Grandpa Jones:

1. Years married?
You: _____ Grandparent(s): _____
2. Number of divorces?
You: _____ Grandparent(s): _____
3. Number of children?
You: _____ Grandparent(s): _____
4. Number of hours (approximate) spent per week enjoying time with family and friends?
You: _____ Grandparent(s): _____
5. Number of evening meals eaten each week at home, with family?
You: _____ Grandparent(s): _____
6. Number of home-cooked dinners per week?
You: _____ Grandparent(s): _____
7. One or more family vacations per year?
You: _____ Grandparent(s): _____
8. Number of household televisions?
You: _____ Grandparent(s): _____
9. Number of hours each week devoted to electronic entertainment (i.e., radio, TV, computer, recorded music, movies, etc.)
You: _____ Grandparent(s): _____
10. Years of formal education?
You: _____ Grandparent(s): _____
11. Number of different jobs held as adult?
You: _____ Grandparent(s): _____

12. Working spouses / two-income families?
You: _____ Grandparent(s): _____

13. Weekends worked per year (approximate)?
You: _____ Grandparent(s): _____

14. Hours spent commuting each week?
You: _____ Grandparent(s): _____

15. Number of different houses lived in?
You: _____ Grandparent(s): _____

16. Number of bedrooms and baths?
You: _____ Grandparent(s): _____

17. Number of years to pay off home mortgage(s)?
You: _____ Grandparent(s): _____

18. Number of cars owned?
You: _____ Grandparent(s): _____

19. Treatment for depression, anxiety, stress, drug / alcohol problems, or related illnesses?
You: _____ Grandparent(s): _____

20. Biggest regret on deathbed?
You (projected): _____ Grandparent(s): _____

Guaranteed Instant Wealth—Just By Reading This!

If you picked up this book thinking that like most personal finance books on the market today, it will offer advice for making more money, maybe even a creative, painless scheme for getting rich quick, you've probably already realized that you'll be disappointed. You probably realize by now that this book is about spending more time taking stock and less time buying stock.

But just so no one is too disappointed, I do have a simple program that will allow nearly every single reader of this book to achieve instantaneous wealth, wealth far beyond the imaginations of most people. If you fit the profile of a typical reader of this type of book, it's as simple as opening your eyes.

By the standards of most people in the world, you are already rich, probably even extremely rich. I'm not talking about the lifestyle you could afford if you could magically transplant yourself with your current income into some remote, undeveloped region of the world; in that case you'd most definitely be a Rockefeller. In fact even many families within the poorest fifth of U.S. households (incomes of $19,178 or less, in 2005) would be well heeled in that imaginary scenario. After all, worldwide nearly three billion people, close to half the people on earth, live on less than $2 a day.

No, I'm talking about the actual, real-time lifestyle and amenities you're currently likely to enjoy and probably take for granted. Little things, like:

- **Housing:** About 1.1 billion people have inadequate housing or none at all, and that's just people living in urban areas of the world.
- **Food:** Worldwide 840 million people are malnourished, and 6 million children under the age of five die every year as a result of hunger.
- **Electricity:** Approximately 2 billion people in the world have none; that's about 30 percent of the world's total population.
- **Water:** Some 1.1 billion people in developing countries have inadequate access to water, and 2.6 billion lack basic sanitation.
- **Education:** Nearly 1 billion adults in the world are unable to read a book or sign their names.
- **Energy:** On average, 1 American uses as much energy each year as 531 Ethiopians.
- **Automobiles:** Worldwide 8 percent of all people own

automobiles; in the U.S. 89 percent of all households own one or more automobiles.
- **World resources:** As much as 30 percent of the world's resources are consumed by Americans, who represent just 5 percent of the world's population.

So how's that for a get rich quick plan? Presto, you're already rich!

My point is not to make Americans, or anyone else, feel guilty, but rather to make us stop and think for a minute about our relative wealth and good fortune from a broader perspective. It's from that perspective that I think you can best begin to understand and incorporate into your own life the concepts and advice in the pages ahead, those things that will help you enjoy life more by spending less.

While guilt is not my intent, I will be challenging you in the pages to come to make a difference. Those of us who have the means to help need to help. Not just help folks in other countries either. Sadly, more than three hundred thousand people in the United States are homeless, and nearly 20 percent of American children live below the U.S. poverty level. Not only can you help people, but you can also help our planet. At our current rates of consumption, within the life span of a child born today we shall deplete the earth's supplies of copper, lead, mercury, nickel, tin, zinc, and—oh, yeah—petroleum.

"Come on now!" you're probably saying to yourself. "Can spending less, being more of a cheapskate, really do all that, and make me happier in my own life too?"

In a word, yes. Or if I can get two words for the price of one: absolutely yes. By spending less on ourselves, we have more—both more time and more treasure—to share with others. By consuming less, we are both leaving more for those who need it and living lighter on the planet. It's just that simple.

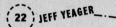
And if contributing to those things doesn't make you happier in your own life, hang on. There's plenty more in it just for you. But I warn you in advance: It's stuff that you can afford only if you're *not* willing to spend the money.

2

Fiscal Fasting:
The First Step down the Road to True Riches

The trouble with the profit system has always been that it was highly unprofitable to most people. —E. B. White

Money, it turned out, was exactly like sex. You thought of nothing else if you didn't have it and thought of other things if you did.
—James Baldwin

Please forgive my husband. He has a spending phobia.
—Denise Yeager's ready response to those caught off guard by her husband's thriftiness

If personal finance writers were doctors, I'd want to be your proctologist. As a kid (less so today) I used to spend considerable time wondering whether you'd recognize a photograph of your own butt if someone showed it to you.

The thought that you might not recognize your own derriere in a lineup fascinates me, almost as much as the thought of a derriere lineup itself. Your caboose is such a large part of you, at least in the case of the Yeager clan. It's something you depend on and use every day, and it's something that's there for everyone else in the world to see, except you. But unless you're a

Cirque du Soleil performer, you lack the perspective (or is it *hindsight?*) to truly come to know your own most enigmatic asset.

And so my proctological aspirations in the field of personal financial advice: I strive to see things from a different perspective, to help you recognize things about yourself that might be apparent to others but may be hard for you to get a clear view of.

Also like a proctologist, I'm a specialist with a specialty, the expense side of personal finance, that is rarely glamorous or pleasing to look at, but one that's extremely important and is too often out of sight and out of mind. In short, I believe that spending money, not making money, is the butt of nearly all our financial problems, worries, and disappointments in life.

That's also why I bill myself as a nonmotivational speaker on the motivational speaking circuit. Other personal finance pundits inevitably seek to motivate their audiences to get more money so that they can spend more money on more stuff. But I'm the guy trying to talk folks in off the financial ledge: "Ma'am, put down your purse, and we'll get you some help"; "Sir, hand me your wallet, and no one will get hurt." My job is to convince you that even if you pull the trigger, even if you spend the money, it won't solve anything or make you any happier.

My premise is simple: Spending less money, skipping the Money Step, is rarely, if ever, a bad thing to do. It's the most personally liberating course of action to become less dependent on money and stuff, and it's almost always the best economic course of action as well.

I believe that thrift can be learned, but it involves a process, a philosophy, a way of life, not just a checklist of ways to save money. So, where do you begin?

Fiscal Fasting: Introducing Yourself to Your Inner Miser

QUESTION: Where does all the money go? I don't recall ever reading a personal finance book—at least one that paid even cursory attention to the spending side of the issue—that didn't include advice (and usually an official-looking worksheet) about charting your monthly expenses so you can better understand where your money goes. That makes sense, since you need to know how you currently spend your money if you're serious about things like controlling spending, getting out of debt, saving money for some special purpose, or adopting a household budget.

Now, do us both a favor and pick up a copy of one of those books by some Master of the Obvious at your local library or download a free spreadsheet from the Internet, and we'll move on to something that really might help you answer the question and change your life forever.

Throughout my adult life I have periodically practiced a financial management technique—almost more of a ritual, really—that I call fiscal fasting. As the name implies, fiscal fasting is the act of denying yourself the use of money for a specified period of time, usually a week or even longer. Yeah, that's right, totally doing without legal tender for the sake of tenderizing your nonmonetary soul.

When I tell people about this penny-pinching pilgrimage of mine, I inevitably get one of two responses:

1. "No way! It can't be done, even for a day. You can't function in this day and age without spending at least some money every day."

2. "No problem! That's easy. I don't spend any money most days anyhow, or at least I don't think I do."

It's the folks who give the second answer who are usually in for the rudest awakening. They're the ones who have absolutely no idea how much cash is passing out of their hands every day, let alone where it's going. But an occasional fiscal fast can be a constructive constitutional for just about everybody, including those of us who have already embraced their inner misers.

Like a traditional dietary fast, the benefits of a fiscal fast include:

- **Purging your system:** Your financial system, that is. Your head will clear, your creativity will soar, and your perspective on life will change when you go money free. And obviously you'll save some bucks during the fast itself, although that's minor compared with the other benefits of fiscal fasting.
- **Tapping your reserves:** By cutting off your intake, you'll start using up reserves of foodstuffs, cosmetics, and other household items you probably forgot you even had. And when it comes to free time and entertainment, you might finally open that watercolor set you bought five years ago after you toured the Monet exhibit.
- **Reflecting and understanding:** Most important, a fiscal fast forces you to think about the impact money has on your life day in and day out. By doing without the convenience and luxury of a ready bankroll, you'll gain insight into your spending habits that no fancy budget worksheet could ever impart. You'll be livin' in a virtual spreadsheet, where you're bound to run into your inner

miser. Who knows? You might even like him once you get to know him; he has a lot to teach you about what's really valuable in life.

Here's How to Play

Sure, you're free to set the terms and conditions for your own fiscal fast, but here are the Official Ultimate Cheapskate Rules for Fiscal Fasting:

1. The fiscal fast should be at least one full week in length, with the starting and ending times determined in advance.

2. Everyone in the family should play. If everyone is not playing, nonplayers are prohibited from interference of any kind, including making purchases on behalf of players or luring them into compromising spending situations.

3. In regulation play, ALL SPENDING IS PROHIBITED, regardless of type of expense (e.g., food, clothing, entertainment, routine bills, commuting costs) or form of payment (e.g., cash, check, charge card, debit card). Yes, in most American households it truly is possible to play by regulation rules! (See Fiscal Fasting Tips and Techniques, on page 30.) However, some families may choose to establish agreed-upon exceptions before starting the fast. For example, commuting costs for working adults or writing a check for the scheduled mortgage payment might be permitted. That's OK if you must, but make sure you agree on the specific spending

exceptions in advance and stick to them. It's better if you can swear off spending entirely and even plan your fast during a time when routine bills don't come due. (Experienced fiscal fasters like me will sometimes up the ante by going without electricity or using other utilities for the week, but that's hard-core play and not recommended for beginners.)

4. No hoarding in advance! Intentionally stockpiling extra food and other supplies prior to the fiscal fast is strictly prohibited and is grounds for disqualification and / or punishment by listening to forty-eight hours of uninterrupted Suze Orman audiotapes. Topping off the gas tank in the family car prior to the start of play is generally permitted.

5. In order to benefit fully from a fiscal fast, during the fast keep a household diary in which all players are required to make at least a short daily entry regarding:

- Challenges of getting through the day without spending any money
- An estimate of how much money they would have normally spent that day, and on what
- An observation (positive or negative) about their fiscal fasting experience that day

NOTE: Despite my rather jaded opinion of worksheets designed to help you track and budget your household spending, I admit that the value of such an exercise is exponentially increased once you have completed your fiscal fast and have this journal for reference.

Recommended Fiscal Fast Reading List

Think you can't do it, go for a week without spending any money? During your fiscal fast, try reading these classic true tales of perseverance, hardship, and spiritual triumph, borrowed for free from your local library, of course. Then see how you feel.

Adrift: Seventy-six Days Lost at Sea (Steven Callahan, Mariner Books, 2002). The title tells you the plot, but the particulars will make you realize just how high on the white shark you're living during your own fiscal fast. Care to go for another ten weeks?

Alive: The Story of the Andes Survivors (Piers Paul Read, Avon, 1975). Airplane crash survivors are stranded high in the snowy mountains with nothing to eat . . . although that dead guy in Seat 27B is looking better all the time. A shocker.

Anne Frank: The Diary of a Young Girl (Anne Frank, intro. Eleanor Roosevelt, trans. B. M. Mooyaart, Bantam Books, 1993). Twenty-five months hidden away from Nazis in a tiny back room apartment, two families depend entirely on the goodwill of others for their meager existence, and those were the *good times*.

Children of the Great Depression (Russell Freedman, Clarion Books, 2005). Written for ages nine to twelve, this is a great family read, but most adults I know need to hear the message—and learn the lessons—at least as much as their kids. Quote: "It's my sister's turn to eat."

Endurance: Shackleton's Incredible Voyage (Alfred Lansing, Carroll & Graf, 1999). Don't turn up the thermostat before you read this one, because after the first few pages you'll realize just how toasty sixty-two degrees really are. The classic tale of Sir Ernest Shackleton's ill-fated Antarctic voyage in 1914. Buuuurrrrr!

Follow the River (James Alexander Thom, Ballantine Books, 1986). This is the true story of pioneer woman Mary Draper Ingles and her incredible one-thousand-mile trek to freedom after being captured by Shawnee Indians. Highlight of the journey: her exultation at finding a single rotten potato to eat along the way.

Into the Wild (Jon Krakauer, Villard, 1996). A young man pays the ultimate price for his lack of planning and preparation. Another one that will make you realize how much food you really have in your "bare cupboard."

The Prize Winner of Defiance, Ohio (Terry Ryan, Simon & Schuster, 2001). OK, so nobody suffers too mercilessly or dies, but maybe it's more poignant because of it. This simple tale of growing up in a household with limited means but lots of heart will warm yours.

Trail of Tears (Gloria Jahoda, Wings, 1995). This is the woeful, true story of the "removal" of American Indians from their native lands in the first half of the nineteenth century by the U.S. government. Hardship, pain . . . and tears.

Voices from Slavery: 100 Authentic Slave Narratives (Norman R. Yetman, Dover Publications, 1999). It's about living without freedom—or much of anything else. Firsthand accounts of freed slaves compiled by the WPA in the 1930s.

Next time you're looking for a New Year's resolution, look no further than your local library. Support your local library and read with your kids. Did I mention it's free?

Fiscal Fasting Tips and Techniques

"Live for a week without spending any money?" I can't do it! I bet you can, and if you can't, it should tell you something even more important about the life you're leading and how you're wasting money.

I remember as a kid being snowed in for five days when a surprise blizzard struck northwestern Ohio one winter. We were without electricity (including heat and running water) the entire time, and we had had no chance to stock up on food and other supplies before the storm. Once the initial excitement of the massive snowstorm wore off and we realized that it might be days before we had contact with the outside world again, even my brother and I were gradually consumed with a mild sense of alarm.

What would we eat? How would we stay warm? What about the disgusting proposition of shitting in a toilet that couldn't be flushed? Most of all, what in the world would we do to entertain ourselves in this cloistered environment, our incongruous family of four, including two gangly teenagers who had recently come to the conclusion that their parents were the dullest, most embarrassing people on earth?

As we fell asleep that first night on the living room floor in front of the fireplace, any feelings of excitement or adventure had long since faded. I remember feeling, well, scared and fairly miserable. I was too old to cry, but not by so many years that I couldn't silently whimper a little bit to myself as I tried to forget about my cold nose and fall asleep. I considered it at the time one of the unhappiest moments in my young life.

Then, five days later, the power came back on, and that truly was the unhappiest moment in my young life. I guess that was the moment when I unknowingly became a devotee of fiscal fasting. What I discovered during those five days—and through all my self-imposed fiscal fasts in the years since—is that getting by with what you have can often be far more fulfilling than getting whatever you want whenever you want it.

FOOD: Despite our initial sense of panic when we realized that we were snowed in that winter without additional provisions, our anxiety began to dissipate as we took an inventory of our kitchen cupboards, refrigerator, and freezer. We were a typical middle-class family, and even though we lived in a rural area, we weren't country farmers who had a meat locker full of beef or a freezer full of farm produce. But we discovered as the housebound days dragged by that not only did we have plenty of food on hand to survive, but as the pickings got slimmer, our creativity blossomed and our menus got even tastier.

In fact the finest meal we had during that five-day siege was on the final night, the night before the electricity came back on. We feasted by candlelight on a long-forgotten package of previously frozen spicy Italian sausage, kept cold in a snowdrift outside the front door and grilled in the fireplace. Mom served it on a bed of canned spinach, pasta, and the last of the sour cream, flavored with garlic cloves roasted in tinfoil over the charcoal embers. My parents even discovered a dusty bottle of homemade elderberry wine in the very back of their liquor cabinet, and we all toasted the long-dead relative who had given it to them many years before. I think that dinner, not just because it was a true Epicurean delight but because of the family warmth and laughter around the table, was one reason why I was not the only one whose eyes welled up when the lights came back on the next day, when we once again had the luxury of getting whatever we wanted whenever we wanted it.

Even though times and families have changed, I still contend that most American families should easily be able to survive comfortably a weeklong fiscal fast on the food they already have squirreled away in their kitchens. If you can't, it's probably because you're eating in restaurants or dining on fast food way too much, or you're not shopping efficiently or cost-effectively for groceries (a later chapter deals with that).

Obviously you'll not be eating out during your fiscal fast, unless you happen across a coupon for something free. You'll be brown-bagging your lunches and putting on your thinking cap when it comes to creative ways to combine the ingredients you have on hand. And you know what? As I discuss in Chapter 4, I'll bet that your family's fare will be more enjoyable than ever, since you'll actually be *thinking* about what you're cooking, not just cranking out the same old recipes.

If you have to break your fast early because you truly run out of food, so be it, but buy only a few staples, not carryout, to see you through. And, as a penalty, you *must* read a selection from the Recommended Fiscal Fast Reading List on page 29 before you throw in the towel and buy groceries. That's just to make sure you understand the difference between a "want" and a "need" when it comes to food.

CLOTHING: If you can't go a week without buying clothes, you have a serious spending problem. If you break your fiscal fast by shopping for clothes, you are in dire need of an economic enema. That's a tough love alternative for those spendthrifts incapable of a self-imposed fiscal fast. (Because of its graphic nature, this subject will be described in greater detail in a later book.)

In fact a fiscal fast is the perfect opportunity to empty out your clothes closet and rediscover all those terrific garments you've forgotten about. Miser Adviser and reformed clotheshorse Sally J. reports that after her first fiscal fast, her subsequent spending on new clothes dropped to near zero for almost a year: "Whenever I got an urge to shop for clothes during the fast, I'd instead pull out a storage box of clothes I already had and try them on. By the end of the week I had so many new—well, new-old—outfits that I didn't feel like shopping for months." Thankfully Sally J. will be spared the economic enema.

SHELTER: The last of the Big Three, food, clothing, shelter. As mentioned before, if possible, schedule your fast for a period when you won't need to make a mortgage or rent payment, helping to maintain the purity of your money-free experience. But also use your fiscal fast as a chance to drill down on and really understand what your shelter is costing you, and ask yourself whether that's a good use of your money. Do some math and record it in your fiscal fast diary. How much is your mortgage / rent on a daily basis? Also, figure out your daily average costs for electricity, water / sewer, heating / cooling costs, property taxes, homeowners' insurance, and other shelter-related expenses.

While you continue to incur these expenses during your fiscal fast, even if you're not writing checks for them, the important thing is to use the fast to begin to understand the true costs of the life you're leading. As a result of undertaking this mathematical exercise as part of my first fiscal fasts, I found that it began to translate into real lifestyle changes and savings. For example, I became much more conscious of the money I could save by conserving water and electricity, not just during fiscal fasts but all the time. And when I used a fast as a chance to dig into my homeowners' insurance policy, I discovered that I could save hundreds of dollars a year by adjusting my coverage and moving the policy to another carrier.

TRANSPORTATION: OK, this can be a tough one to abstain from, particularly if you have work-related commuting costs like gasoline, parking, tolls, and bus fares. But sit down and really think about it before you say it can't be done. Also, skip ahead to Chapter 6, which deals with transportation, and read Chris Balish's book *How to Live Well Without Owning a Car* (Ten Speed Press, 2006), then see what you think. Can you carpool with coworkers during your fast, or walk or ride a bicycle to work? Is telecommuting an option? Again, even if you decide to exempt commuting costs from your fiscal fast, use it as an opportunity to figure out what transportation is really costing you—car payments, insurance, gasoline, maintenance, etc.—and ask yourself if it's both truly necessary and worth it. And if your kids are used to driving or being driven to school, it's time to reacquaint them with either the school bus or their bicycles—no exceptions.

BUT WHAT ABOUT———?: You name it, and you can do without it or find a substitute for it during your fiscal fast. Cigarettes, booze, lottery tickets? Use your fast to kick your habits, at least for a week. Cosmetics and toiletries? Try rationing what you have; there's enough shampoo in one of those little hotel-supplied bottles to wash the average male head of hair every day for a week. Household cleaners? When all else fails, try baking soda (see page 113). Paper products? Use real cloth napkins, dish towels, and old rags—not just during the fast but to save money and the environment year-round.

ENTERTAINMENT: You don't need to spend money to have fun, as you'll see in Chapter 8. In fact, if you break your fiscal fast by giving in to spending temptations intended to keep you entertained, I'm willing to bet that you're someone who ultimately leads a very unhappy, unfulfilling life, despite your spending. Am I right? If so, don't despair, but keep reading; by the end of this book I hope you'll find your own on-ramp to the Highway to Happiness.

If for no other reason, the impact a fiscal fast can have on your family's entertainment choices and spending patterns makes the exercise worthwhile. Case in point: Miser Adviser Doug M. says that his family rediscovered "together time" and "simple pleasures" during their first fiscal fast, to the point where they now regularly impose an entertainment only fast on the weekends, a way of forcing the family to dream up free, fun things they can do together.

"If we let ourselves buy movie tickets, inevitably everyone goes their own way at the multiplex. Same thing with going to an amusement park or renting videos or giving the kids their own fun money. The options that involve spending money seem to discourage time together, not encourage it," Doug M. says. "Just the things we've found buried in our garage—fishing poles, ice skates, a badminton set, you name it—have given us days of free fun time as a family. If you limit yourself to using what you already own, it makes you think and actually inspires you to do more, things you'd never think up if all options are available. I think everyone in the family would agree that our best weekends are the ones where we say to ourselves, 'We're not going to spend any money on entertainment this weekend.' That's pretty ironic, isn't it?"

I'm not surprised, as I learned during my original, involuntary fiscal fast that Ohio winter. By the end of the five days my brother and I were beginning to see our parents in a different light. Maybe they weren't as dull or embarrassing as we thought. After all, Mom even spelled out F-A-R-T when we were playing Scrabble (only seven points, but ten solid minutes of howling laughter), a word we never thought she even knew, let alone would ever use. And as we huddled around the fireplace to keep warm, Dad told us a cool, true story about the time Grandpa Yeager single-handedly apprehended a knife-wielding purse snatcher on the street of New York City, an image hard for us to fathom given the staid grandfather we'd always known.

Even after we dug out from the snowstorm, and electricity,

running water, stores filled with limitless supplies, and the convenience of spending money reentered our lives, our family always seemed a little closer because of the experience. Something stuck in the back of my mind, sandwiched in between the image of my *Charlie's Angels* poster and the memory of the toast we all shared with that elderberry wine: "Maybe less really can be more."

✎ EXERCISE: Conduct Your Own "What the Hell Was I Thinking?" Audit

One of the most valuable management exercises I developed during my tenure in the nonprofit sector came to affectionately be known as the "What the Hell Was I Thinking?" Audit by my staff.

At an annual retreat during budget time, each manager was asked to share with the group his or her top spending regrets, the biggest budgetary boners, of the fiscal year just ending. I would start off by confessing mine, with staffers gladly chiming in if they thought I'd left anything out, and then each would perform his or her own self-confessional in front of a room full of eager critics.

The purpose wasn't to embarrass or demoralize anyone—in fact the spirit was all in good fun—but rather to learn from our own mistakes and those of our coworkers. Not only did it achieve that objective, but it cultivated a more open, less defensive attitude about finances throughout the year. As a staffer once told me during the year when I raised an eyebrow about a dubious purchase he was proposing, "You're right! Come September, I don't want to see this one on my 'What the Hell Was I Thinking?' Audit."

Years ago I adapted this technique to my personal finances. Although a solitary exercise (yes, even I'm gun-shy about asking my wife to participate), I find that it's still both a constructive and therapeutic exercise, *constructive* in that I always identify some expenses—rather "mistakes"—that I won't make again, and *therapeutic* in that the more years I perform the audit, the fewer spending snafus I identify. Think of it as spending quality time with your inner miser.

A fiscal fast is the perfect time to perform your "What the Hell Was I Thinking?" Audit, since you're already meditating on money anyhow. And it really doesn't matter whether you audit your monetary missteps annually or just every so often; just start from your last audit, and go from there. Here's how:

1. *Create a spreadsheet:* Set up a card table in your living room and cover it with butcher's paper (or tissue paper, in a pinch), like when we eat blue crabs here in Maryland. You're going to need some elbow room (like when we eat blue crabs here in Maryland) and something to write on (other than a lotto ticket, like when we eat blue crabs here in Maryland).

2. *Compile your financial records:* Gosh, I get a little constipated just hearing those words. Don't sweat it. Just dump out whatever credit card statements and canceled checks you can find without sweating it. (I bet if this little exercise turns you on, you'll find that next time around you'll be able to lay your hands on those records without breaking a sweat.)

3. *Highlight the low points:* Now, using a highlighter pen (or, better yet, a bingo dauber if you own one), breathe deeply and ask yourself one question: If I had it to do over again, would I buy that? Highlight the expenses you regret on your credit card or bank statements, and make a note of those purchases (items and amounts) on a corner of your butcher paper spreadsheet.

4. *Determine corrective actions (if applicable):* Although the primary purpose of the audit is to recognize and learn from your erroneous spending patterns, ask yourself if it's still possible to correct your mistakes. Can you still return an item for a refund (remember, more and more retailers have very liberal

refund / exchange policies; see Chapter 3)? Can you sell an item in the classifieds or give it to a charity or someone else who will appreciate it? If you're dissatisfied with the results in the case of misspent funds for services like home repairs and improvements, is it too late to approach the vendor about a partial refund or even to lodge a complaint with the Better Business Bureau (www.bbb.org)?

5. *Analyze the audit results:* Once your What the Hell Was I Thinking? list is complete, take a few minutes to look at it more carefully. Do you see any patterns in your misspending habits? Do you tend to regret certain types of expenses (e.g., clothing, technology, meals out) more often than others? Do you regret purchases from some stores more than others, or do your spending missteps increase certain times of the year or when you're stressed out at work?

Since you have a card table covered in butcher's paper, make a note of any misspending patterns that emerge, and formulate some resolutions around those trends (e.g., "I will wait at least thirty days between the time I see a new video game in the store and when I buy it, just to make sure I really want it"). Save your butcher paper spreadsheet to refer back to throughout the year, and use it to compile a What the Hell Was I Thinking? list to carry in your purse or wallet at all times (see Chapter 3).

He's Not Cheap; He's My Grandpa

Ever since I was dubbed the Ultimate Cheapskate, people have asked, "Were you raised cheap, or did you become a cheapskate all on your own?"

That question has given me pause to reflect on my family and upbringing, an enjoyable, free, and rarely indulged exercise in and of itself. As a result, I've come to realize that I truly come from frugal stock, an undeniable family bond.

Like many American families, the Yeagers have spent considerable time tracing their genealogy, hoping, like many American families, to discover some compelling, momentous, maybe even history-changing facts related to their ancestry. What brand of manifest destiny inspired the Yeagers of old to uproot themselves from the peaceful German countryside and strike out for the uncertainties of the New World? Was it a quest for *freedom*? *Riches?* Or maybe even *love*?

No, it was *insurance.* Much to the amusement and delight of my good-humored father, Doug, who spent his whole career working in the insurance field, a great-aunt's exhaustive research resulted in a most unspectacular finding. My great-great-great-granddad Yeager came to America to collect on a life insurance policy that was due the family as a result of his brother's dying in the Civil War. As my father says, "I just always knew that claims adjusting was in our blood."

Looking back on it now, I see that Clyde Yeager, my grandfather, had the miser gene in spades. A diehard do-it-yourselfer and a recycler of things that anyone else would have thrown away without hesitation, Clyde was definitely my biological grandfather. There's no need to do a DNA test.

Growing up, we just thought him a bit eccentric. But in retrospect he had a special gift when it came to thrift-craft.

Clyde was a highly skilled, self-taught carpenter, mechanic, plumber, electrician, farmer, butcher, barber, and landscaper, with a basic understanding of veterinary medicine that allowed him to experiment on two-legged beasts as well. His skills paid off during the Depression, when his homemade toolbox got him the nod as the sole hire out of an employment line of more than two hundred out-of-work men. It also paid off throughout his life, as he built, repaired, rebuilt, and reused.

I never remember my grandpa and grandma Yeager *ever* paying anyone to do anything for them, beyond their charitable "hiring" of their young grandsons to help out with Clyde's endless projects. They'd built and entirely paid for their comfortable two-story house before they were even married, thus never knowing the pressures of meeting a mortgage a single day in their lives.

A friend of mine once observed about me, "Jeff's never met a piece of scrap lumber he doesn't like." Oh, but if he'd only known my grandpa Yeager.

Clyde was such a passionate saver of scrap materials that eventually storage became a problem. I remember one summer when a tornado ripped through northern Indiana, where my grandparents had a small summer cottage (which of course they had built themselves). The storm picked up a floorless steel storage shed in their backyard and deposited the twisted metal carcass in a nearby tree. Miraculously, the contents of the shed remained perfectly intact in the backyard, having been packed so tightly from floor to ceiling that at first glance it looked as if the shed had survived unscathed.

Clyde was also one of the great diluters of his time. He reasoned (and I suspect he was at least partially, if not entirely, correct) that the manufacturer's instructions for virtually every product would have you use far more of the product than is truly necessary. After all, manufacturers have a vested interest in the accelerated consumption of their products, don't they?

Clyde, determined to fight back against this consumer scam, set out on his own campaign to dilute the potency and / or reduce the recommended dose of products of all kinds. Milk, juice, household cleaners, salad dressings, ketchup, and bottled sauces and condiments all were cut with water. Medicines were often taken in partial doses, detergent amounts were reduced by half, and chili ordered in a diner was stretched by use of the ketchup bottle on the table (double bonus: The ketchup was free, and it wasn't even watered down). Even pricey eggnog at the holidays was cut with less expensive Coca-Cola, which, believe it or not, is really pretty tasty and still the way I prefer mine today.

Most of all, Clyde had a special relationship with linseed oil, not just as a diluter for paint, varnish, and other mineral-based products, as it's intended, but as a preservative and lubricant of almost all worldly objects. To hear Clyde talk, linseed oil was God's gift to mankind. Its restorative and preservative qualities knew no bounds.

He applied it to leather, wood, rubber, canvas, concrete, and anything and everything metal. I remember standing outside his house during a spring shower and marveling at how the water droplets beaded up and rolled off everything in sight—the tarp over the boat, the picnic table, the sidewalk, the overturned wheelbarrow, the Buick LeSabre. Ah, the power of linseed oil.

Clyde's passion for linseed oil had a downside, though. He himself regularly took on the sheen of the substance, resulting in a mandate by Grandma Yeager that he always sit on a bath towel when relaxing in his favorite easy chair. Eventually the towel too absorbed the linseed oil. In the winter of 2006 I was glued to the TV watching the Winter Olympics in Torino, Italy. In between coverage of bobsledding and Alpine skiing, NBC ran a fascinating story on the mysterious Shroud of Turin, the ancient piece of fabric said to contain an image of the crucified Jesus.

"Déjà vu," I said to myself, "just like the Shroud of Clyde!"

3

Six Golden Rules for Ruling Your Gold

*i am living so far beyond my income that we may almost
be said to be living apart.*   —e. e. cummings

STOCKS WON'T SINK AS BOOMERS RETIRE, U.S. SAYS—
(WASHINGTON) *A congressional investigation released
yesterday has discounted any danger that a wave of
retiring baby boomers will cause a precipitous decline in
the stock market by suddenly selling off their financial
assets. The Government Accountability Office's report
concluded that most boomers have few assets to sell. . . .*
—wire service report, reprinted in the *Toledo Blade,*
July 26, 2006

Remember, friends don't let friends pay retail.
—the Ultimate Cheapskate

I don't spend a lot of time Googling myself, at least not in the
more recent sense of the term. But with my recognition as the
Ultimate Cheapskate I occasionally go online to see what's being said about me in various money-related chat rooms on the
Internet.

I'll tell you up front that some of the buzz has been pretty
negative about me and my approach to money, but then you
need to consider the source. If one more middle-aged guy hud-

dled at his computer screen at two-twenty in the morning calls me a jerk, I'll personally pay his overdue bill at the *Privates* of the Caribbean Web site so that he can get back to the real reason he's telling his wife he suffers from insomnia.

Here's a typical posting from one of those late-night one-handed typists: "What a jeeerk!!! This loser should just get a real job like everybody else and stop being such a schlockmeister! It's un-American!"

Fair enough, that's one point of view. BTW, I had a "real job" for many years. My point is that there's another way, a way to lead a full, satisfying, happy life without always needing to go through the Money Step, the act of earning and spending money. As for my being "un-American," my approach is clearly less materialistic, but the founding fathers embraced and revered the cheapskate ideals of providence, frugality, and conservation. As Thomas Jefferson wrote, "It is neither wealth nor splendor; but tranquility and occupation which give happiness."

Admittedly some of the things I do are a little extreme, at least for the fair-weather cheapskate. Like trying to weave a sweater out of dryer lint (one of the great untapped resources of our time). Or my lifelong passion for cushion mining, stealthily fishing around for lost change in the cushions of hotel lobby furniture (trust me, those things are like upholstered ATMs). And yes, I save the airsickness bags (unused, of course) from when I fly to use as lunch bags or, if I'm feeling romantic, to place on the dinner table with a candle inside, a cheapskate luminary that would make Martha Stewart a little nauseated (unless she didn't know its origin, in which case she'd think it was a "very good thing").

But just in the last week I saw a piece on TV about "man purses" costing seven hundred dollars each, an ad for an eight-passenger minivan with sixteen cup holders, and a news item about designer "lifestyle dog foods" with, for example, flavor en-hancers specifically developed for chihuahuas. So I ask you, who's the extremist? Who's the loser? What happened to the prudential virtues of our country's founders?

And the Nobel Prize Goes to . . .

If there was a Nobel Prize for Cheapskate Economics, I'm con-vinced that my theory of Contra Economics would land me a laureateship. Contra Economics is my hypothesis that the vast majority of the American economy consists of corresponding, nonsensical spending transactions that effectively cancel each other out. My research suggests that if you were to adjust for the effect of Contra Economics, the actual size of the U.S. econ-omy is slightly smaller than that of Lithuania.

For example, Americans spend roughly $2 billion every year on unwanted hair removal (e.g., electrolysis, bikini waxes) and about $2 billion annually on promoting hair growth (e.g., Rogaine, hair transplants). I guess the good news is that as a na-tion we believe we have the right amount of hair. The bad news is location, location, location.

Just look around. Other examples of Contra Economics abound in our world of unending spending. While each might not exactly offset the other, collectively you get the point:

- U.S. sugar industry: $10 billion annually.
  U.S. sugar-free industry: $5.7 billion annually.
- $10 billion annually in the United States on cosmetic surgery.
  $600 million annually for online dating service. (You'd think that after $10B in plastic surgery, we'd at least

have enough self-confidence to meet people face-to-face.)

- Total energy used in producing a twelve-ounce can of diet soda: 2,200 calories.
  Total food energy in a twelve-ounce can of diet soda: 1 calorie.
- U.S. candy sales: $24 billion annually.
  U.S. dentistry industry: $69 billion annually.

And this final example of Contra Economics has me particularly worried: It costs taxpayers *at least* $180 per coyote to exterminate those animals under a government-sponsored program of aerial gunning. Even more (up to $800 per creature) if there's a lower concentration of coyotes in an area (www.coyoterescue.org). At the same time, coyote urine, prized by U.S. gardeners as a deer repellent, sells for a whopping $22.99 for a mere twelve-ounce bottle (see www.PredatorPee.com).

Despite my exhaustive research, I've been unable to determine how much urine an average coyote generates (it's apparently a yellow area of the sciences). But twelve ounces strike me as very little, as proved out by some home experiments I've conducted using my own bladder and a measuring cup. Regardless, I'm quite certain that a dead coyote does not produce urine.

So, rather than kill the coyotes, we should capture them and force-feed them light beer, thereby driving down the cost of coyote urine, even if the cost of capturing versus killing the animals is somewhat higher. My concern is simple: If left unchecked, the cost of coyote urine will continue to rise as the population of coyotes dwindles because of aerial gunning, making extermination efforts that much more costly, and round and round we go. Pretty soon the entire U.S. economy goes down the drain or, at best, is reduced to a trickle.

I definitely feel a laureateship coming my way.

A Goal You Can Live With

So call me cheap, but a jerk? I have too much competition from the earn-spend-earn-spend crowd for that title. I'm content to think of myself and my views as a tiny piece of ballast against the overwhelming majority sentiment of our day: Get more money / buy more stuff.

I don't for a minute think that everyone will embrace his or her inner miser to the extent I have, but that's OK. Unlike most plans promising personal financial salvation, part of the beauty of my spending-centered approach is that even if you take only a small part of my advice or do a half-assed job of it, you'll still come out ahead.

How's this for a mantra you can live by? "Today I shall do at least a piss-poor job of using the Ultimate Cheapskate's advice."

Do it and I guarantee you'll see real results. How many other personal finance plans can make that claim?

When it comes to advice, in my experience there's:

- Stuff written on public restroom walls
- Suggestions
- Guidelines
- Tips
- Hot tips
- Rules
- Stuff written on private restroom walls
- And of course golden rules

If your attention span is limited and / or you're reading this in a public restroom, the following is just for you: my Six Golden Rules for Ruling Your Gold or, as I prefer, my Six Gold Nuggets. By understanding and incorporating these money principles in your life, you'll be taking control of your spending and freeing yourself from the stranglehold money has on most people. You'll be well on your way down the Road to finding True Riches.

GOLD NUGGET No 1: Live Within Your Means at Thirty, and Stay There

If there's one golden rule revealed in this book that is of a higher karat than all the others, it's the simple one stated above. Simple to understand, that is, but not so simple for most people to live by, unless of course you've already slain your *Enoughasaurus*.

It's about avoiding one of the great modern-day financial pitfalls: allowing your expenses to rise to meet or even *exceed* your income. It's about establishing a permanent standard of living, one that's both comfortable and affordable, rather than constantly chasing an escalating standard of living. It's about not becoming dependent on a salary and lifestyle that might be unsustainable or, in the end, unsatisfying.

When I was first starting out in my career, making all of ten thousand dollars a year in an entry-level position with a nonprofit organization, I thought a lot about how much more money I would need to earn each year to afford the things I wanted. As my salary gradually grew with annual pay increases and promotions, I decided around the time I was twenty-five or so that if I could ever make forty thousand dollars a year, I would be the happiest man alive. I would then be earning enough to afford everything I wanted or at least everything I thought I wanted at that point in my life.

I didn't know it at the time, but the day of that epiphany I struck a lethal blow to my *Enoughasaurus*. The raging beast didn't succumb to the wound for some years to come, but the mortal damage had been done. I had set a fixed amount, a fixed amount of what I wanted in life and a fixed amount of money that it would take to get it. For me, on that day, money and the quest for money stopped being relative and instead became a tangible goal I could work to achieve. It was no longer just about getting *more*; it was now about getting forty thousand dollars a year.

I freely admit that on that day I felt absolutely no sense of profound enlightenment or breakthrough. In fact I wasn't even aware of the existence of *Enoughasauri* at that point in my life. But I did remember and stick to my $40K catechism.

Over the next few years my salary continued to increase, and Denise and I married; our combined incomes met and then began to exceed my forty-thousand-dollar benchmark. And you know what? On that day—again, not a specific day, but at that point in my life—I truly was the happiest man alive, just as I'd thought I would be.

As we settled into our new life together, I shared with Denise both my feelings of total contentment and my vow about living grand on forty grand.

That's when I first met her *Enoughasaurus*.

"Gee, *honey*, I'm so glad that you're thinking about our finances and all. It really makes me feel secure. But you know, we already make more than that, and we're just starting out. Certainly we can afford to spend more than that, can't we?" she said.

"Well, *sweetie*, sure we can afford to spend more than forty thousand a year, but that's not the point," I said gently. "I just realized one day that that's all I'd ever need or, well, all we'd ever need, to be happy. Not that I'm trying to decide for you or anything, I just—"

"But, *sugarplum*, how are we going to be able to buy a house and afford to travel and do the other things we've talked about doing on such a tight budget? Besides, you even admit that we can afford to spend more than that," she added, now with a twinge of insistence in her voice.

"*Cupcake,* you know how much I love you, and you know I want us to be happy and be able to do all the things we've talked about doing. It's just that I think it's a mistake . . . and unnecessary . . . to always spend everything you make." As I spoke, Denise started rubbing my thigh, and it was clear she'd had enough of our little financial debate, content at least for the time being to let it drop. We concluded the first money match of our marriage in the way newlyweds often do.

I know that Denise's *Enoughasaurus* didn't even flinch that day. In fact I swear I could hear her beast snickering with each loving platitude we exchanged. But time was on my side.

A couple of years later, when Denise grew miserable in a job that grossly underutilized her abilities, she bemoaned the fact that she couldn't just quit.

"I'd turn in my resignation tomorrow if we could afford it!" she said in utter frustration.

"Why don't you?" I said. "You know we haven't been living on your salary anyhow."

"What?" she said. "What do you mean?"

I went on to share with Denise a little secret I'd been keeping: that in reality we'd been living pretty much on just my salary and the rental income generated by the one-bedroom guest apartment attached to the house we'd bought the year before. After all, that totaled roughly forty thousand dollars a year. Gee, where had I heard that figure before?

While I don't condone keeping secrets from your spouse, in this case my revelation was greeted with tears of relief, appreciation, and a little disbelief. Needing to be further convinced— I tallied up our monthly expenses on a scratch pad—Denise realized that I was in fact speaking the truth. Her salary had essentially been going either into savings or into making additional principal payments on our home mortgage. Without her salary we wouldn't be able to continue to fund those activities, but the good news was that we wouldn't have any change in the quality of our life if she resigned her position.

"Thank you," she said, "I feel so much better now." Now, a few years into our marriage, I initiated the thigh rubbing.

It turned out that Denise's job environment improved and she decided to stay in her position, in part, as she said, because she knew that she always had the option of resigning, knowing that nothing awful would happen to us financially if she pulled the plug. Denise's *Enoughasaurus* hasn't reared its ugly head since.

Living within your means is only common sense, but drawing a line in the sand early in life—establishing a permanent standard of living for yourself and your family when you're still relatively young—is truly a life-changing power play. Refusing to become dependent on an escalating lifestyle and income is one of the most valuable financial assets you can have, and it doesn't cost you a dime. Whether it's forty thousand dollars a year or some other amount, or whether it's your lifestyle at age thirty or some other age, the important thing is to slay your *Enoughasaurus* by establishing a limit and sticking to it.

If you set your targeted standard of living early enough in life and at a comfortable but not excessive level, you're likely to accomplish three things that will fundamentally shape your relationship with money for the rest of your life:

- **Automatic savings plan:** Because your income is likely to increase throughout your working years, by capping your spending at X dollars and banking the rest, you've set in motion an automatic, painless savings plan.

Saving is no longer a matter of cutting back on something; it's just a matter of staying the course, of continuing to enjoy the standard of living you've established.

- **A comfortable, sustainable lifestyle, even in hard times:** By establishing a permanent standard of living as we did, if you lose a job or encounter some other financial emergency, your lifestyle is likely to remain constant rather than decline or even collapse. It might not be possible to find another high-paying position like the one you lost, but you don't need to in order to continue to lead the life you've been enjoying, because you haven't become dependent on that higher income for your standard of living.

- **Peace of mind:** Ah, the biggest reward of all. People think that being "cheap" means always thinking about money. But just the opposite is true. Once you've settled on what's enough for you, you can stop thinking about it and get on with enjoying life. May your *Enoughasaurus* rest in peace.

You may be wondering whether Denise and I continue to live at the forty-thousand-dollar level this many years later. In all honesty I must tell you no, we do not. After we paid off our house early (see Chapter 5), we found that without a mortgage payment, forty thousand was in fact more than we really needed to continue to enjoy the lifestyle we'd always enjoyed. Now we live very comfortably on twenty-five to thirty thousand dollars a year, which is roughly equivalent to our original $40K standard of living, less the mortgage payment and adjusted for inflation.

As for our *Enoughasauri*, the last we knew they took a vow of poverty and are living happily together on an island off the Horn of Plenty.

EXERCISE: Look Who's Hitting on Your *Enoughasaurus*: Conducting Your Own Reverse Focus Group

Slaying your *Enoughasaurus*—deciding what is "enough" for you and then designing your priorities and life around it—is hard enough without an interloper from outside. You need to take stock of what you already have and do some real soul-searching about what you truly want out of life. And you need to recognize the true costs and implications of the Money Steps you'll encounter along the way.

Fortunately the pages ahead will help you do all that, but first I mentioned an interloper. Well, not just one. More like three thousand. And that's three thousand every day.

That's how many advertisements researchers say Americans are exposed to each and every day. During the course of your lifetime you'll spend about an entire year just viewing television commercials.

I became interested in advertising when I was thirteen. Well, maybe more like *fixated* on advertising. That's when I overheard my older brother and some friends discussing the fact that there were images of naked women hidden in the photographs of cornflakes on the Kellogg's box. They said companies did it all the time to get you to buy their products; it was called subliminal advertising. I called it a miracle.

I raced to the kitchen, grabbed the box of cornflakes, and scurried back to my bedroom to conduct a thorough examination. But no matter how much I squinted or how I turned the box, I just couldn't see anything other than cornflakes. I once thought I saw a nipple, but on closer inspection it was a smudge off the price sticker.

Yet to this day I, the Cheapest Man in America, must restrain myself from picking up a box of Kellogg's in favor of the less expensive store brand when I shop for cornflakes. Coincidence? Subliminal advertising? Wishful thinking?

Before you can rein in your *Enoughasaurus,* you need to understand its weaknesses, its passions, its *triggers.* That's why professional marketers conduct what they call focus groups. Unlike broad-based marketing tests and surveys that involve hundreds or even thousands of people, focus groups do just that: They focus on the perceptions, tastes, and reactions of a select few, believing that they'll learn more from these detailed encounters than from superficial mass samplings.

The good news is: If you want to battle back against the bombardment of advertisements you're exposed to every day, you can conduct your own reverse focus group. After all, you're the only market sample that really counts when it comes to your own spending habits, right? You and your experiences / opinions are all you'll need. Give it a try.

How Easy Are You?
Use these questions to determine how easy a mark you are for marketers and to identify areas where you need to strengthen your resistance. Give yourself one point for every question you answer yes to:

_____ I rarely or never buy generic or house-brand products.

_____ If I knew for a fact that the exact same product was in two different packages, one my usual brand and one generic, I'd still be willing to pay more for my usual brand.

_____ I've purchased an item that I didn't want, simply because I found the person selling it (a live salesperson or in an advertisement) sexually attractive.

_____ I can sing the jingle from the advertisement for the car I own.

_____ When I see a brand-name product shown in a movie, I'm not aware of the fact that it was almost certainly placed there by a paying advertiser.

_____ I've purchased something from a telemarketer.

_____ I've purchased something from a late night infomercial.

_____ I've purchased something from a pop-up ad on the Internet simply to make it go away.

_____ I wear adult diapers during the Super Bowl so I don't need to leave
          my chair for a potty break and miss any of the commercials.

_____ I watch QVC regularly.

_____ I never watch PBS because it's commercial free.

_____ I believe that advertisers are providing a public service by
          educating consumers about their products.

_____ I do not consult *Consumer Reports* before making major purchases
          because I think it is biased (not to mention there are no
          advertisements in the magazine).

_____ I have a child who shares the same name as a product I use.

I can name the brands associated with the following slogans /
phrases (one point each):

_____ "We love to fly and it shows."

_____ "I can't believe I ate the whole thing."

_____ "For the time of our lives."

_____ "Can you hear me now?"

_____ "We answer to a higher authority."

_____ I believe that at least most of the time an advertiser is being
          truthful when it uses the words "sale" and / or "new and
          improved."

_____ I've purchased a product that claimed to give me any of the
          following without serious exercise and / or surgery: six-pack abs,
          buns of steel, bigger breasts / penis (or both).

_____ I can distinctly recall at least one commercial I saw the last time I
          watched TV.

_____ I've cried during a Hallmark card commercial.

_____ I've been in an auto accident because I was trying to copy down
          information from a radio advertisement while I was driving.

_____ I can recall the contents of one or more roadside billboards I
          currently pass on my way to work.

_____ I can see images of naked women embedded in the pictures on the Kellogg's cornflakes box (no points, but if you can, please send me a sample carton with the images highlighted. Thanks).

20–25 points: Yikes! You need immediate help. Have you considered entering a convent?

15–19 points: Trouble zone. Without corrective action, there's a 50 percent chance you will eventually sell advertising space on your body to the highest bidder.

10–14 points: Average American.

5–9 points: Nice! You're in control of your buying decisions more than most, and I bet your household budget will verify it.

0–4 points: Congratulations! You've succeeded in inoculating yourself against the power of most advertising. (What rock is it that you live under, again?)

OUT OF SIGHT, OUT OF MIND

Five things you can do to help edit advertising out of your life:

1. Record TV shows on tape to watch later and fast forward through the commercials.

2. Listen to tapes and CDs rather than commercial radio.

3. Install spam filters on your computer.

4. Sign up for the National Do Not Call Registry to prevent telemarketers from calling (www.ftc.gov or call 1–888–382–1222).

5. Declare April 1 your annual No Fools Day. Use it to contact companies that send you unwanted catalogs and other junk mail and tell them to stop it—_now_.

GOLD NUGGET NO. 2: Never Underestimate the Power of *Not* Spending

Spending less money is rarely, if ever, a bad thing to do. Sounds simple, but let's really think about it for a minute. Is it possible that *not* spending money is a far more powerful tool for achieving financial freedom than all the books ever written on the subject of how to make more money?

I can see you're skeptical, as you should be. And I'll admit up front that there are some legitimate examples of when spending less money *is* a bad thing to do, like being "penny wise and pound foolish" and forgoing routine maintenance costs on your home or car, which may mean that you have to spend more in the long run for major repairs. Fair enough. There are some exceptions, but only a few.

Of course lots of times you hear people say, "You need to spend money to make money," and that is patently false. Most people make most of their money by selling their time, not by investing or leveraging their money or using it to launch some type of entrepreneurial enterprise.

However, my counteraxiom—"You need to spend money to *lose* money"—is in fact very close to being a universal truth. Short of your losing wealth as the result of being robbed or involved in some unfortunate accident or other situation out of your control, money is lost only as a result of your *choosing* to invest it or otherwise place it at risk or, more commonly, to spend it on something that eventually becomes worthless. Therein lies the true power of *not* spending.

People—at least people with money—are obsessed by the return on their investments (ROI). "How did our Dreyfus Premier Greater China Growth Fund fare against our Matthews Korea this quarter, darling?" "Why would I lock up any money in a six-month CD when six month T-bills are paying 5.09 percent?" "Sure, she's our daughter, but what kind of ROI can we expect if we loan Buffy the hundred thousand she needs to start her dog biscuit bakery?"

"ROI" is part of lots of people's vocabulary and, sadly, their dinnertime conversation. But you rarely hear about the other option, what I call return on noninvestment, or RONI—that is, the true net effect of your choosing *not* to spend money or to spend less than you would normally.

RONI of course isn't a new idea, even though you don't hear anyone talking about it these days. Remember "A penny saved is a penny earned," per Ben Franklin?

While I have tremendous admiration for Franklin and his succinct words of wisdom, with all due respect, it's really more like "A penny saved is equal to approximately 1.3 to 2.0 cents earned, when you factor in taxes and other costs you are likely to incur on an earned penny, compared with a saved penny." That's no joke. A saved, unspent penny is worth considerably more than a penny you need to go out and earn; that is why understanding RONI and the power of *not* spending is so important and a first step in embracing your inner miser.

Most people are as naive about calculating the true returns on their noninvestments as they are about calculating the much more scrutinized and discussed returns on their investments. In my experience, people commonly tend to *overestimate* the returns on their investments, in part because of wishful thinking and in part because of the complexity of calculating fees, taxes, the cost of the money they're investing, and other factors. At the same time, most people clearly *underestimate* the returns on their noninvestments, if they stop to think about them at all.

As I constantly reminded those who worked for me in the organizations I managed, the easiest and cheapest dollar we'll ever make is the one we don't spend. That's not only because of taxes owed on the earned dollar, but because of the costs you're probably incurring to earn that dollar in the first place, particularly if you subscribe to the "spend money to make money" philosophy. Examples of those costs in your personal life probably include everything from commuting costs, meals eaten out, and a special wardrobe, if you're a working stiff, to inventory carrying costs, investment losses, and depreciation expenses, if you're a business owner.

But believe it or not, those are actually the easiest, most apparent factors to take into account when determining the true return on the money you choose *not* to spend. The really tough ones—and arguably the most valuable—are the intangible benefits that are generated by not spending that dollar, again, the "enjoy life more" parts of this book. To paraphrase Ben one last time, you need to realize: A penny saved is a penny you don't need to earn again.

How will you use the extra time freed up by not needing to earn that extra dollar? How will not needing to earn that dollar improve things like your health, your relationships with others, your life satisfaction? How much would you be willing to pay for those extra few minutes when you have only a few seconds left on this earth?

One final point about the importance of RONI versus ROI makes me think about the way birth control methods are rated for their effectiveness. As I recall from Coach Sacstretcher's eighth-grade sex ed class, there is a clinical effective rate and an actual effective rate of birth control methods.

"Clinical" describes the effective rate under ideal, clinically controlled conditions, which seems to me a rather ridiculous (although interesting to imagine) calculation. For example, I suppose the withdrawal method is 100 percent effective in the clinic, since it is, by definition, the act of withdrawing before you release the sperm necessary to induce pregnancy. But the "actual" effective rate, as the name implies, is based on what's likely to happen in real-life situations: "Gee, I swear I pulled my dilly whacker out in time, just like Coach Sacstretcher told me to!"

It seems to me that personal finance gurus should be required to use a similar clinical versus actual rating system when dispensing financial advice. For example, the U.S. stock market has a proven historical compound return of about 10.7 percent annually (the clinical success rate). But if you followed the advice of so many financial advisors and initially invested in the market in early 2001, you're likely to be still reeling from your actual success rate (although, yes, you still got screwed).

I hope you've anticipated my point. When it comes to RONI—return on noninvestment—the clinical and actual success rate is the same. By choosing not to spend the dollar, you know with absolute, 100 percent certainty that you will still have the dollar and the luxury of not needing to earn that dollar again. That is the power of not spending.

Having the Time of Your Life

You've heard it over and over again, and you've probably even said it yourself: Time is money.

And it's true. Most people make most of their money by selling their time, not by investing, winning the lottery, or some other extraordinary means. Unless you're born into wealth or stumble onto it, the greatest financial asset most of us have is our time because we can sell our time in exchange for money. So time truly is money in that sense.

But it's the antithesis of that adage that weighs heavily on this miser's mind: Money is time. If you spend your time making money, you'll no doubt have more money. But if you don't need so much money, it also follows that you'll have more time, more time for other things, other than making money.

Let's face it, while money is limitless and in that sense relative (as discussed earlier), time is limited and finite. We have only so much of it, so how can anyone argue that money and the stuff you can buy with it are more precious than time?

This simple but underappreciated observation is key to understanding how skipping the Money Steps can transform your life. It gives you back your time, time to spend with family and friends, time to spend pursuing your passions and helping others. If in the pages ahead you find yourself thinking that you just don't have the time to take some of my advice for skipping the Money Steps (to do your own home repairs, shop for the best bargains, go for a weekday hike, read to your kids, volunteer at a local homeless shelter), BINGO! that's the point: Time is money *but* money is time. If you spend less money, you'll have more time.

Now, I'll fight you if you question my thriftiness, but not my intelligence. In fact this whole philosophy of life and personal finance is not a product of my own creative genius but was pioneered by Joe Dominguez and Vicki Robin in their 1992 must-read book *Your Money or Your Life: Transforming Your Relationship with Money and Achieving Financial Independence* (Penguin, new ed., 1999).

Trained in finance and economics, the authors walk readers through a series of financial calculations and other exercises designed to help you evaluate what you're really selling your time (or life energy, in their words) for and whether it's worth the trade-off. They write:

> Our life energy is our allotment of time here on earth, the
> hours of precious life available to us. When we go to our jobs
> we are trading our life energy for money. This truth, while

simple, is profound. Less obvious but equally true, when we go to the welfare office, we are trading our life energy for money. . . . So, while money has no intrinsic reality, our life energy does—at least to us. It's tangible, and it's finite. Life energy is all we have. It is precious because it is limited and irretrievable and because our choices about how we use it express the meaning and purpose of our time here on earth.

And speaking of our time here on earth and how we choose to spend it, I suggest looking at the *2007 Statistic Abstract of the United States* (www.census.gov/compendia/statab/). Despite its lackluster title, it is guaranteed to shock and awe. Here's how we Americans, on average, are spending the time of our lives:

- Commuting to / from work: 202.5 hours annually
- Sitting motionless in traffic commuting to / from work (metro areas): 42 hours annually
- Taking work home with us: reported by 49.3 percent of office workers
- Watching TV: 43.2 solid days / 1,036.6 hours annually (up 39 percent since 1960)
- Volunteering / civic / religious organizations: 1.8 days annually
- Caring for children: 1.5 hours a day (down 40 percent since 1965) . . . or a little less than half the time we spend watching TV every day

GOLD NUGGET NO. 3: Discretion Is the Better Part of Shopping

The other day I saw a home organization expert on TV who claimed that 80 percent of all nonperishable items we buy are either underutilized or entirely unused. His contention was of course that if we are more organized, we can maximize the use of our purchases. Fair enough, but if those statistics are even remotely accurate, they confirm what we all already know: We buy a hell of a lot of stuff that we rarely or never use. In most cases, the goal shouldn't be to find a way to use it; the goal should be to find a way not to buy it in the first place. After all, if we own something but never use it, certainly our quality of life will not suffer if we skip the Money Step and avoid the purchase altogether.

I've noticed that most people have some things they openly express regret about buying as well as a special collection of things tucked away in the back corners of their closets that only they know about. These latter are the things that are so nonsensical, so embarrassing, so hideous that you've never fully admitted even to yourself that you were addlebrained enough to buy them in the first place. These are the kinds of purchases you have nightmares about. But when you suddenly wake up with a sense of "it was only a dream" relief, you know better than to actually look in your closet.

For me, it's a half dozen plug-ugly sports coats that I've amassed over the years, what I fondly call my Nausea Collection. One is a key lime green sports jacket I bought thinking that it would make me the stud double of Don Johnson in *Miami Vice*. Instead, every time I've ever worn it and happened into a Wal-Mart or other discount store, I'm instantly approached by customers requesting my help in locating the Metamucil or other hard-to-find items on the store shelves.

Apparently the jacket makes me look so much like a Wal-Mart management trainee that I now just go with it, confidently instructing my fellow shoppers that they'll find fiber supplements on Aisle 5, next to the Depends.

To the best of my knowledge, I am the only researcher working today to develop a vaccine against buyer's remorse. So far my efforts have fallen short of this ultimate goal, but I have run across some other prophylactic methods to help curb impulse buying until we develop a fool-proof vaccine:

- Establish a mandatory waiting period, your own personal Brady bill, when it comes to discretionary spending. Spending procrastination—putting off until tomorrow what you could buy today—is a virtue, not a vice. I suggest waiting at least one full week between the time you first see an item in a store and the time you go back to buy it. If you're anything like me, more than half the time you'll either forget about it, decide you don't want it, or decide you want it but never get around to going back to buy it. I've also found that even if I do make the trip back to the store after the mandatory waiting period, I often change my mind when I see the item again. If you're afraid that an article of clothing won't be available later in your size or that some other potential purchase will disappear, rediscover the once coveted art of layaway, the stock option of retail. For a small, usually refundable deposit, you can reserve an item for purchase at a later date—if you don't lose interest first. As my great-aunt always said, "I'd rather put something on layaway than lay awake nights wondering how I was going to pay for it on a credit card."

- Make a What the Hell Was I Thinking? list, and carry it with you at all times. Use a three-by-five index card (which can be folded into business card size to fit neatly in your wallet / purse) to make a list of recent purchases that you already regret. Next time you get ready to make a discretionary purchase, take a few moments to read through your What the Hell Was I Thinking? list, and maybe you'll decide to pass. "Nausea Collection" is the first item on my list, followed by that set of electromagnetic nipple clips I bought online that promised to reduce the size of my male breasts—ouch!

- Pay with cash, not by credit card or debit card, for a month, and see how your spending drops. Depending on the extent of your plastic addiction, it may be best to chop up your credit cards altogether, but a one-month trial separation is a useful exercise for anyone who ever uses a charge or debit card. By forcing yourself to count out actual greenbacks when you go to buy something, you'll be surprised how much thriftier you'll become. According to various sources, people are inclined to spend significantly more when paying by credit card rather than with cash, including up to 30 percent more for the exact same item—now that's lucre lunacy. Psychologically, it's a lot harder to part with dead presidents than to whip out the plastic. Plus, you need to plan ahead to have the cash on hand, so you might find yourself with a cooling-down period that will make you think twice.

- If you're going to shop with friends, shop responsibly: Appoint a Designated Cheapskate. Most shopaholics will tell you that their disease is exacerbated when they shop with a group of other like-minded spendthrifts. Susan B., a recovering shopaholic who is now one of my Miser Advisers, confirms that peer pressure and a mob mentality prevail when friends shop together. "It's hard enough to control it [wanton spending] when you're by yourself, but when you're with a group and everyone is enjoying themselves and buying stuff, you just go along with the group without even thinking about it. Pretty soon you have one of everything anyone else bought, plus shopping bags full of your own things," she says. If this sounds familiar, when you shop with a group, try appointing a designated cheapskate, someone who agrees not to make any purchases of his or her own and instead serves as the voice of reason by cautioning others about impulse purchases.

- If you slip, save the slip—the sales slip, that is. This is not so much a prophylactic measure as a morning-after pill. One of the few changes truly benefiting U.S. consumers in recent years has been the proliferation of no-questions-asked return and exchange policies. Once relatively rarely, now most major retailers, and smaller stores as well, will gladly refund your purchase without even asking for an explanation, although most still require you to produce a sales receipt within a specified refund period. Clearly retailers have decided that it's better to retain you as a happy customer in the long run than to lose your future business by refusing you a refund. (Being the jaded consumer I am, I also think that the general deterioration in the quality and attitudes of retail sales employees has ironically helped facilitate hassle-free exchanges. Most store workers couldn't care less about the customers, whether they're buying something or returning something. The salespeople just want to process the transaction and go on break.) So save your sales receipts, and don't be afraid to return those impulse purchases (for a refund, not an exchange!) when buyer's remorse sets in. Are you embarrassed about returning items? Great! If you force yourself to do so, the chagrin you feel may actually have a therapeutic effect and help you curb future impulse buying. Beware, though, more and more retailers are tracking your refunding habits and cracking down on habitual refunders by cutting them off.

- And here's a really effective one: Volunteer for a few hours every month at a local homeless shelter; then see how you feel about buying some more stuff. See Chapter 8 for more info on volunteering.

Where the Cheapskate Shops

Where to shop for what is the subject of great debate and speculation among cheapskates and other economizers. But I don't think it's really that complicated or debatable.

A few simple rules have always served me well. Like: I buy new clothes only at stores that also sell pork chops in bulk. So-called big-box membership warehouse stores consistently have the best prices on casual apparel for men. And if you're a guy like me who hates to shop for clothes, the bonus of shopping at big-box stores is lack of selection. They generally have just one or two styles / brands to choose from (but in three different colors!), so there's nothing to think about and keep you from wheeling your flatbed shopping cart over to the meat aisle or, better yet, the display of hydraulic jacks two aisles over.

Here's my take on different shopping venues:

Boutiques: French for "small stores with big prices."
Supermarkets: The best prices on groceries are inevitably the

store specials offered by each chain, usually listed in a weekly flyer in your newspaper and / or on the chain's Web site. Cherry-picking—buying just the top sale items at each chain (usually listed on the front page of the flyer)—is generally the way to go, provided that you don't burn up your savings in gas by shopping the different chains. Fortunately, the big chains are making cherry-picking easier by knocking down our last few neighborhood woodlots to build their stores closer and closer together; my goal is to cherry-pick them out of business and save a ton of loot in the process. In most parts of the country, warehouse-style supermarkets (i.e., bag your own grocery stores with somewhat more limited selections, but not "jumbo-sized" packaging or membership requirements like the big-box stores, below) are the most economical choice for everyday grocery shopping, if you're not a cherry picker.

Convenience stores: Perfect places to shop when the world is about to end and you're looking for the last scraps of nourishment and supplies before the four-headed guys from the starship scarf it up. Otherwise, never shop there.

Ethnic markets: Don't overlook neighborhood Hispanic, Asian, Middle Eastern, and other ethnic markets in your quest to bag some grocery bargains. Not only will you broaden your culinary horizons by checking them out, but many everyday staples—rice, beans, meats, vegetables—are less expensive in ethnic markets where customer demand for certain items is high. Also check out the international food section of your regular supermarket for savings on spices and other foreign-brand items being sold for a lot more in the next aisle over.

Farmers' markets: Twenty years ago farmers' markets were fun and frugal places to shop. They're still fun, but the bargains aren't what they used to be. Nowadays you'll usually pay a premium for produce and other food items purchased at most farmers' markets, although freshness and quality might make it worth the price. If you're looking for bushel quantities to do some canning, there can still be good values at many farmers' markets, or better yet, find a pick-your-own farm in your area at www.pickyourown.org.

Department stores: A dying breed. Why? Because even their big sales suck when compared with other choices. Good news: Their going-out-of-business sales might be OK.

The marts: You know, Wal-Mart, K-mart, Target, etc. Not bad for everyday household items, clothing, and the like, but quality-wise you can usually do better for the price on housewares and clothing at smaller national and regional chains like TJ Maxx, Marshall's, and Filene's Basement. If you like the marts, then you're ready to gradu-ate to the Holy Trinity: dollar stores, big boxes, and thrifts.

Dollar stores: For cheapskates, the emergence of dollar stores over the past decade or so has been our stem cell research, some-thing new with tremendous potential, but not without its contro-versy. Some of my Miser Advisers rail against them, citing items like paper products, soda, and other food items as no bargain at a dol-lar, since you can consistently find them on sale for less (per unit) at grocery stores. Then there's the tendency to buy things you really don't need, since "it's only a buck." But I'm a dollar store devotee, keeping in mind that not all dollar stores are created equal. There are half a dozen national dollar chains and a growing number of local mom-and-pops. Not everything at some stores (e.g., Dollar General stores) is a dollar, although that's the practice at my favorite stores (e.g., Dollar Tree and Dollar King). And since most stores deal in dis-continued and overstocked merchandise, stock can vary from store to store and day to day. A number of recent consumer surveys have shown that it's hard to beat dollar stores when you shop for a wide range of items, including toiletries, cleaning supplies, snack foods, kitchen accessories, gift wrapping, greeting cards (two for a dollar), and party supplies. And Miser Adviser Cindy W. writes: "Where else can you give your kids a dollar apiece and tell them they can buy anything in the store? Our local dollar store has two full aisles of toys and novelties. My kids get as much joy out of a one-dollar shopping spree as they would a twenty-dollar one. It's the experience that counts, not the amount."

Membership warehouse stores (aka big-box stores): There are seventy-five million card-carrying members of America's big-box behemoths (e.g., Costco, Sam's Club, BJ's), which says something about their value. You know the downside, *big* quantities, so make sure you have the storage space, and watch perishables for spoilage. But the upside is significant: in nearly every instance, lower per unit costs than you'll find even when a product is on sale elsewhere. Plus, the quality of meats and produce at big-box stores tends to be a superior restaurant grade, and many products (e.g., cleaning supplies, paper products, furniture) are also heavy-duty industrial strength. Moreover, the positive side of the jumbo packaging is that you'll save even more money by shopping less frequently. As for the membership fee (usually twenty-five to fifty dollars annually), do the math; most customers easily recoup the fee in just a couple of visits.

Thrift stores: Don't be shy. Secondhand stores run by Goodwill, Salvation Army, and other nonprofit groups aren't just for the economically disadvantaged; these organizations depend on shoppers of all economic means to patronize their stores and help them raise funds by liquidating donated merchandise. Different stores tend to have different specialties (e.g., clothing, furniture, home accessories). Many stores have special sale days, and most are open to negotiating for better prices. Office furniture and equipment (including computers) are real bargains, since many businesses donate hardly used items in order to keep up their cutting-edge image. TIP: Shop early in the week for best selection, following weekend clean-out-the-garage donations.

Tag sales and auctions (live and online): More of a hobby than a practical way to shop since you never know what you'll find where. But if you have shopping fever, they're a good and less expensive catharsis, and you can find some real treasures that might even make you a few bucks.

Shopping malls: Crack houses for shopaholics. Repeat after me: "If I *must* shop at all, it will *not* be at a mall."

GOLD NUGGET NO. 4: Do for Yourself What You Could Have Others Do for You

I am, like most of my cheapskate brethren, a diehard do-it-yourselfer. From all types of home repairs and remodeling to automotive maintenance, appliance repair, landscaping, interior decorating, catering, and even self-administered haircuts, there are few, if any, projects that I won't tackle on my own. As I tell my wife, "I approach every job as if it were my first" . . . because many times it is.

I so loathe paying anyone to do anything for me that my wife is convinced I'll find a way to bury or cremate myself upon my demise. Why not? There's no greater opportunity to avoid the Money Step than to do something for yourself instead of earning the money to pay someone to do something for you. Again, it's not about sacrifice. In the end, the life experience you gain by learning to do something for yourself is even more valuable than the money you save, and you still get the same end result.

But the money you save shouldn't be underestimated. Labor costs are, almost by definition, the majority of any bill issued by the "service industry." During my year-end "What the Hell Was I Thinking?" Audit (Chapter 2), I specifically break out—and inevitably bemoan—any amounts I pay others to do things for me. What if you could just do *everything* for yourself and skip all those Money Steps?

I became so enamored with the do-it-yourself movement that in the early 1980s with the popularization of home video rentals I was convinced that we were on the cusp of a revolutionary new era of DIYism. I believed that we would soon see a world where everyone would pretty much do everything for himself or herself. With high-quality instructional videos that could be played and replayed in our own homes and the right set of tools from our local rental centers, I believed we would essentially eliminate the need to pay other people to do things for us.

I knew from firsthand experience that fixing a leaky sink was relatively easy with a how-to book from the library and my trusty set of wrenches. If you could rent both a detailed how-to video and the necessary tools from a single store, think how easy it would be and how much money you could save. Then my mind really started clicking.

I predicted that within a year or two people would be making their own clothes, styling their own hair, cooking their own gourmet meals, even treating their own psychoses. Why stop there? With the right tools and a detailed instructional video, home surgery had to be right around the corner, I reasoned. Start small—mole removals, ingrown toenails, maybe a vasectomy—before moving on to the major stuff. And if the videotape malfunctioned midoperation, home embalming had to be a no-brainer.

Alas, just as I was glimpsing what I thought was a new frontier of doing things for yourself, the opposite was happening. As my wife says, "Jeff, sometimes I don't know if you and your ideas are ahead of the pack or you just got lapped."

Depsite the fact that Home Depot is now one of the thirty megacompanies that constitute the Dow Jones Industrial Average and that other national "home improvement" chains have edged out smaller competitors, traditional DIYing appears to be on the decline. The backbone of these national retailers' business is sales to the trade (i.e., contractors that perform the work for others) and sales of nonconstruction consumer items, like furniture, appliances, carpeting, gardening supplies, and plants. And installation services offered by these do-it-yourself stores are a burgeoning profit center.

If you're a fan of *This Old House* and other home improvement shows on TV, you know what I mean when I say that real DIYing is on the decline. It used to be that these shows actually showed you how to do things for yourself and on a limited budget. In fact I am a proud DIY graduate of the *This Old House* of old, owing most of what I know about home repair and remodeling to professors Bob Vila and Norm Abram. But now these shows have devolved into an explanation of whom you need to hire so they can do the work for you, without any mention of a budget or spending limits.

Ironically, as the world has become more complex and we increasingly depend on others to do things for us, the reality is that it has never been easier to do most things ourselves. Gone are the days of real craftsmen, lifelong practitioners who mastered the skills and acquired the knowledge that separated them from novices. Now the guy they send over to fix your toilet, resurface your driveway, or even build your new addition—you know, the guy with his butt hanging out like two giant portobello mushrooms—is likely to have little more training, experience, or knowledge than you do.

As a result of a decline in skilled labor and / or maybe precipitating it, product manufacturers of all kinds have worked to simplify the installation, maintenance, and repair of their products. It's now true that any idiot with the right tools can do almost anything, with or without the requisite pair of portobellos.

While this is the reality of the situation, you'd never know it from the marketers employed by the service industry, whose job it is to scare us into thinking we can do nothing for ourselves. We *must* go through the Money Step: Earn the money to hire someone to do something for us rather than simply do it ourselves. But with Ebenezer Scrooge as my witness, I vow to you that you can do far more for yourself than you think you can, if you'll only try. And there's no greater sense of personal satisfaction than accomplishing something that you once believed you could not.

Here are a few DIY tips and observations to consider:

- **Tools:** Having the right tools is at least as important as having the right knowledge, and with those two commodities skill is overrated and success is all but guaranteed. To limit frustration, make sure you have the necessary tools and other supplies on hand before you start a project and that you know how to operate the tools by practicing as necessary. Refreshingly, unlike so many products today, the quality, durability, and capabilities of tools (both hand and power) used for construction and mechanical projects tend to increase directly with price. With few exceptions, there really aren't "designer" tools, for which you pay extra just for an in name or a trendy design. For the most part, you get what you pay for, and when it comes to tools (and hardly anything else), I'm a big believer in buying the best that you can afford. The life expectancy of the tool and the quality and ease of the work you perform with it will more than make up for the extra expense in the long run. And by making the front-end investment in good-quality tools, you're likely to tackle more projects yourself.

- **Maintenance:** If you're new to DIYing, start by learning how to maintain what you already have—your house, car, bicycles, appliances, lawn mower, etc.—rather than jump immediately into major repair or remodeling projects. This will allow you to become familiar with how things work and how to use tools, and as experienced DIYers know, it's also where you'll save the most money in the long run. In short, take care of your stuff, and your stuff will take care of you.

- **Pacing:** One of the most common mistakes made by DIY newbies is to start multiple projects simultaneously or to fail to set priorities. In part, this is a testament to how exciting and empowering it is once you start to realize that you can actually build / repair / create things yourself. But it's destined to get out of hand; with unfinished projects everywhere you look, it's easy to become discouraged and waste money through unused supplies and temporary fixes. I draw up an annual schedule of major projects I want to undertake and then divide it into four quarterly schedules that also include routine and smaller projects (e.g., tuning up the lawn mower) and unexpected things that pop up. It's common for novice DIYers to underestimate the time involved in completing a project (and, to a lesser extent, the expense), but your estimating skills will quickly improve with experience. Another nice thing about home improvement projects is that with many projects there seems to be a natural balance between the pace of your work and your cash flow; it's possible to pay for the materials and supplies you need as you go.

- **Know-how:** Despite the fact that my how-to-perform-surgery-at-home videos have yet to make their way to the shelves at Blockbusters, another lesser invention has helped to fill the void. Not only has the Internet made how-to-do-anything information widely available (check out www.eHow.com and www.howstuffworks.com), but product manufacturers now commonly make their installation, maintenance, and repair instructions available online. This latter feature is invaluable for all of us who have long since lost the instruction manual for the vacuum cleaner we bought in the late nineties, the one that now needs a new belt. Couple that with the resources available for free at the library and (my favorite) the inexpensive how-to courses offered at local community colleges, and in no time at all you'll be at least as knowledgeable as old portobello buns.

GOLD NUGGET NO. 5: Anyone Can Negotiate Anything

In countless cultures around the globe it's considered poor business—even downright unfriendly—*not* to bargain or negotiate when purchasing goods or services. While we don't have that economic tradition here in the United States, I think you'll be pleasantly surprised if you give it a try next time you go shopping. I think you'll be surprised at how much money you can save simply by asking for a discount, and I think you'll be even more surprised at how—once you get the hang of it—it actually makes the shopping experience more satisfying and enjoyable.

Of course many Americans are uncomfortable about asking for discounts and about the process of negotiating in general. We're embarrassed to ask for better prices or to haggle over other terms. But what most Americans don't know is that even in the United States retailers are usually open to negotiation.

Mom-and-pop stores are used to it, and even major retail chains are increasingly empowering their sales staffs to cut better deals in order to build customer loyalty, maintain customer satisfaction, or just make the sale. Management and sales staffs frequently have authority to match sale prices (their own and / or their competitors') or simply discount items up to 10 to 20 percent at their discretion.

So how do you ask? There are books written about the art of negotiating, most of them by high-powered businesspeople with big bank account balances offered up as proof of their deal-making skills. But I'm not aware of much written on the topic by nonprofit guys, let alone cheapskates like me.

That's surprising, because negotiating is a way of life in the nonprofit world and a point of personal pride among cheap-skates. And unlike the Donald Trumps of the world, we in the nonprofit sector negotiate out of need, not greed, and we rarely have the luxury of negotiating from a position of power. In these ways, I think skilled nonprofit managers have a lot more prac-tical negotiating advice to offer regular folks than rich and fa-mous businesspeople do.

If nothing else, those of us in the nonprofit world have to be-lieve that *absolutely everything* is negotiable. As I used to tell my staff, most of whom were initially sheepish about bargaining with vendors, just think of themselves as being "honor bound" to ask for a discount or constantly push for a better deal.

I used to tutor green staffers in the art of negotiating by coaching them in what I called reopening the can of worms— that is, periodically approaching vendors with whom we had ex-isting, binding contracts and asking them point-blank to reopen negotiations for the express purpose of giving us a better deal. Because we asked nicely and based the request simply on the position that we would prefer a better deal than the one we had agreed to earlier and because we never threatened or made un-true allegations of failings on the vendors' part, our forthright, bold approach nearly always brought the other parties back to the table when they could have just as well hidden behind the existing contracts.

As a result of the years I spent with charitable organizations, I came to realize many important things about negotiating and deal making:

- Everything is in fact negotiable.
- If approached correctly, negotiating can build stronger, more positive partnerships, even friendship, and need not be contentious or lead to strained relationships.
- Even the most hesitant, inexperienced person can become an effective negotiator and, to his or her surprise, learn to enjoy the process.

Obviously these professional experiences and skills quickly found their way into my personal life. Because of my willingness and ability to negotiate, I would estimate that I trim, conservatively, 5 to 10 percent off our annual household spending.

I ask for a "nice guy discount"—a discount based on no rationale other than the fact that I'm "a nice guy"—on nearly everything I buy, and I would say that about a third of the time I receive some concession in return. Then there are the big-ticket items, like furniture, travel, and major household purchases, where I really go to work and typically expect to improve the original offer by at least 10 to 20 percent.

Here are my top three negotiating tips if you're new to the world of bargaining or shy about the process:

- **Never, ever, go first.** This is the single most important rule if you're negotiating for something when the terms of the transaction (especially the price / cost) have yet to be established. My staff used to kid me that my bladder, which knows no bounds, is my greatest negotiating tool. I can and will wait an eternity for the other party to *go* first when it comes to defining the initial offer (not to mention rush to the bathroom). You can usually goad the other party into firing the first shot by professing ignorance ("Gee, I'm so new to this I

wouldn't even know where to start") and / or appealing
to his or her ego ("You're the expert at this; help me
understand what's a good deal") or both. As a last
resort, you can always walk away from the table—or
threaten to—unless the other guy shows you his first.
Whether you're buying a car or a house or negotiating
some other contract, in my opinion you can only lose
ground by being the first one to propose a price or other
negotiable terms. By your waiting him out, the worst
that can happen is that the other party throws out some
terms that are way off from what you want / expected, in
which case you enthusiastically object. But in many
cases you'll be surprised when the other party comes out
with an initial proposal that is as good as or better than
what you expected, in which case you can only trade up.
You run a tremendous risk of selling yourself short by
going first, and there's no downside to forcing the other
guy to go first, provided that your bladder can hold out.

- **Always negotiate from a position of *nice*.** This flies in
  the face of all the conventional wisdom about always
  negotiating from a position of strength, but it's the
  reality most of us live with, certainly in the nonprofit
  sector, where we're usually the weaker of the two
  parties. Regardless of your position going into a
  negotiation, I truly believe what Teddy Roosevelt once
  said: "The most important single ingredient in the
  formula of success is knowing how to get along with
  people." To be friendly, polite, attentive, and well
  mannered throughout the negotiating process is not
  only the high road, but is likely to be the most direct
  road to the best deal. There's a saying among
  professional fundraisers—"People give to people"—that

applies to all forms of negotiations, not just the act of asking someone for a charitable contribution. Never fool yourself; it's always good to be nice.

- **Never on a Monday.** This is a simple, painless tip if you're uncertain about your negotiating skills: It's not about what you do or what you say when you negotiate; it's just about when you do it. I have always believed that the best, easiest deals are made late in the week, particularly on Fridays and especially on Fridays right before three-day weekends. This is true of all types of deals—purchases as well as resolutions of unpleasant issues. It stands to reason that earlier in the week folks are generally in a bad mood and have resigned themselves to the fact that they must toil away the entire week on the work before them. No one is motivated to make a deal, to wrap anything up. All that changes as the weekend approaches. Salespeople want to conclude the week by closing sales, so you get a better price. The guy you've been arguing with at the insurance company about your claim doesn't want to ruin his weekend by thinking about a pain in the ass like you; he's ready to resolve the claim. In fact, look at my deal with Broadway Books to publish this book: inked on a Friday, right before a three-day weekend.

GOLD NUGGET NO. 6: Pinch the Dollars, and the Pennies Will Pinch Themselves

If I hear one more financial pundit tell me I can put my financial house in order simply by giving up a four-dollar cup of Starbucks coffee every day, I'm going to force him to listen to his own audiotapes while I show him photographs of Suze Orman's face photo-shopped onto Halle Berry's body. As painful as that would be for me, that's how strongly I feel about striking down such nonsensical advice; I'm fully prepared to sacrifice what's left of my dwindling libido for the cause.

The so-called Latte Factor and that whole genre of "save big money painlessly" plans are flawed in a number of ways, starting with the fact that lots of us are way too smart to pay four dollars for a cup of coffee in the first place.

But then again, guys like me just can't bring ourselves to order anything with a silly-sounding name, no matter how much it costs. When I order a cup of coffee, I want to be able to say "a large cup of coffee, please." Even if I were inclined to shell out four dollars for a cup at Starbucks, guys like me would rather shit their pants in public than suffer the embarrassment of saying something like "a grande caffe latte, please."

The math behind these pseudo savings plans is valid enough, I suppose, usually involving multiyear projections to show how small daily savings can add up over time. When you factor in theoretical earnings on those theoretical savings, pretty soon you can theoretically retire. But as discussed earlier, in birth control lingo those are undoubtedly the "clinical" results, while the "actual" results are likely to be much different.

These types of painless savings schemes appeal to the same people who want to believe that they can get abs of steel by wearing magnetic belts. I seriously question both the effectiveness and practicality of these plans, and I'm not sure that in the end they're even that painless. I'm also concerned that the pundits who preach these plans are ultimately doing a disservice to their congregations by not leveling with them about the real choices involved in securing financial freedom, even if those choices are less appealing.

So why, in real life, are these latte factor type of fad savings diets likely to be so ineffective? For one thing, if it's not an amount of money you think twice about spending in the first place, it's not an amount of money you'll think twice about saving either. Sure, theoretically, small, single-expense savings over a long enough period of time can really add up, but as a practical matter each savings transaction is so small it will most likely be absorbed and spent on other equally trivial items. In real life it's too easy for the four dollars you saved by not buying your latte this morning to morph into an extra pizza topping this evening.

Because each of these savings transactions lacks what I call critical financial mass (i.e., sufficient financial size to be meaningful to most people), I bet that they'll never see the inside of a bank vault even if you manage not to turn around and spend them on extra pepperoni. In real life who has the discipline to bank four dollars at a time and invest it continually, since latte factor projections inevitably assume continually compounded investment returns on your daily savings? Oh, sure, put your four bucks in a special pickle jar on your bedroom dresser every evening until you've reached some critical financial mass, but the next time you need twenty bucks to pay the paper boy on a Saturday morning, I bet it's the gherkins that'll pay.

And are these flavor-of-the-month painless savings schemes really all that painless? If you've ever been on a diet, you know that each time you consciously deny yourself something to eat, no matter how small the potential treat, that act of denial makes its mark. Could it be that a small daily sacrifice might in fact be more painful, not less, than making a single fundamental lifestyle decision?

Just as most health experts emphasize lifestyle change over diet as the most effective way to get fit and stay fit, so I believe that by concentrating on even one or two of life's major Money Steps (mega-expenses like those we shall be looking at: housing, transportation, technology, entertainment, and health), you can set yourself on a worry-free financial course for the rest of your life.

It's also important to understand fully the potential financial impact of major decisions we make in our lives, even those decisions we make more from our hearts than from the financial lobes of our brains, things like having children (about $200,000 per child, birth to age eighteen; see www.Bankrate.com); marrying and then divorcing (which can easily reduce your standard of living by half to two-thirds or more; see www.divorcesupport.com); or even owning a pet (about $780 yearly for a mid-size dog; see www.aspca.org). NOTE: These Web sites provide calculators that allow you to make more precise estimates based on individual variables.

If you're wise enough to grapple with these Money Steps early in life, money can become a relatively inconsequential aspect of your life. And because you've made the right big decisions or even a couple of them, the small decisions won't make or break you.

In the remainder of this book we'll look at some of these fundamental lifestyle-based spending decisions in greater detail. Keep in mind that these are the decisions everyone *must* make one way or the other, the decisions that truly cast the die when it comes to your relationship with and dependency on money. Do as I suggest, and maybe you can even have a grande caffe mocha frappuccino every morning, just so long as I don't have to order it for you.

Put Your Finances on Autopilot

Most people would be well advised to heed this paraphrased warning from Jack Nicholson's character in *A Few Good Men:* "The money? You can't handle the money!"

Today's world of automated banking and finance has some real downsides for those trying to get their financial houses in order. Cash is quickly becoming an antiquated novelty, making the concept of money, and going into debt, more of an abstraction than ever before. And with the speed and ease of transferring and spending money online, at an ATM, or over the phone, it's easy to lose track of your true financial condition. As a young colleague of mine said, "The ATM keeps spitting out bills, so I must be in good shape."

However, other modern-day banking conveniences—what I call financial autopilots—can actually set you on a course for financial independence. Here's how:

- **Start with direct deposit.** Out of sight, out of mind. Make arrangements to have your paychecks and any other routine payments you receive deposited directly into your bank account. You remove the temptation of cashing your check at the bank and deciding to splurge with a night (or three) on the town. You also save time, and time is money, particularly since this is a free service offered by nearly all banks and employers.

- **Consider splitting your deposits.** But don't stop with simply having your paycheck deposited directly into your checking account, out of which you probably pay most of your monthly bills. Instead, sit down and figure out what other automatic allocations you can make of incoming funds. As your budget allows, make arrangements to have a portion of each paycheck deposited directly into a savings account, for example, or even into various special savings / investment accounts set up for your kids' college tuition or an emergency fund. Not only does this institutionalize your savings plans, but if you're investing in stock or bond-based funds with each paycheck, it means you'll automatically be dollar cost averaging, the term for reducing the risk of buying high by investing on many different days rather than all at once.

- **Now put your routine bills on autopilot.** Once you've made arrangements to put your incoming funds on autopilot via a direct deposit plan, turn your attention to your expenses. Make a list of your routine monthly bills (e.g., phone, electric, insurance), and contact those vendors to arrange for those bills to be paid automatically out of your checking account each month. This usually involves your filling out an authorization form and supplying a voided check for the account from which the payments will be withdrawn. Nearly all vendors offer direct pay plans, free of charge. This saves the time and expense of writing monthly checks and eliminates the possibility of incurring late fees. You'll continue to receive copies of your monthly bills, so you can check them for accuracy. To simplify my cash flow and make sure I always have enough on hand to cover these automatic withdrawals, I've set up just for these direct pay expenses a special interest-bearing checking account, in which I try to maintain a comfortable cushion of two or three months' worth of funds.

- **Don't forget credit cards and the mortgage.** Two of the most important financial autopilots most people should consider setting up are automatic payment plans for their credit cards and home mortgages. By making arrangements with your credit card companies to automatically pay off your balance each month, you not only avoid late fees and interest charges but ensure that you won't rack up insurmountable charge card debt over time. Obviously it takes financial discipline to make sure that you're able to cover these automatic debits to your account, but it's the second best way to handle your credit cards (first, of course, is a pair of scissors). And by all means contact your mortgage lender and authorize it to deduct your payments automatically; after all, if you have a mortgage, payments aren't exactly optional. Most mortgage lenders even offer a supercharge autopilot, the so-called accelerated payment plan, discussed and recommended in Chapter 5.

- **Don't sweat it; just do it.** Stop wringing your hands and worrying about whether you'll be able to handle all these bills being deducted directly from your account, and just set your finances on autopilot. You'll be surprised at how once these systems are in place, you'll worry a lot less about money and you'll establish a comfortable income / expense routine. And direct pay plans can usually be discontinued or modified quickly, with a simple phone call if you should need to do so.

There's nothing wrong with admitting you can't handle the money!

4

Warning: Money May Be Hazardous
to Your Health

*NOTICE: We are overstocked and no longer accepting
donations of used exercise equipment (even if never
used). —The Management* —sign of our times posted in the
Clinton (Maryland) Thrift Store

*If you have health, you probably will be happy, and if
you have health and happiness, you have all the wealth
you need, even if it is not all you want.* —Elbert Hubbard

*If you are what you eat, then I should be reduced for
quick sale.* —the Ultimate Cheapskate

Pick up a magazine, watch the evening news, or shop for a self-
help book, and you know that money and health / fitness are
the two great obsessions of our time. Oddly enough, we don't
usually think of these two obsessions as being connected, and
when we do, we see it back-ass-ward. We believe that we need
money—lots of money—not only to be happy but to be healthy.
From eating a nutritional diet to joining a health club to hiring
a personal trainer, it takes money to get and stay fit, right?

Wrong. In fact there's good reason to think that just the opposite is true. Other than allowing for the cost of medical health care, could it be that there is actually an inverse relationship between having money and enjoying good health? Could it be that money is hazardous to your health? Or maybe more accurately, that money is an enabler, something that helps encourage unhealthy lifestyle choices?

I'm not just talking about money as an enabler of poor health in the obvious sense—that is, that money makes it possible for us to ruin our health with traditional addictive substances like cigarettes, drugs, and alcohol. Those are of course important health issues in their own right (smoking alone costs the United States $157 billion annually in health care costs and lost productivity) and arguably ones that are ravaging our society like never before because at least in part, we are better able to afford them than ever before. We can now afford not only to support our vices but to support treatment for our addictions and to fund those industries that pour billions of dollars into advertising designed to encourage our relapse, a spiral staircase of Money Steps, if you will.

No, as important as cigarettes, drugs, and alcohol are when it comes to health issues of our time, I want to focus on the exercise and dietary choices everyone makes every day. Specifically I want to look at how by choosing to take the Money Steps when making these choices, we may be taking steps away from good health, not toward it. At the very least we're spending money unnecessarily, when we could instead skip the Money Steps (or greatly reduce them) and go straight to the prize—in this case, good health.

The reality is that almost without exception, the healthiest choices you can make in life also happen to be the least expensive. Adding to the irony is the fact that the more money you have, the less likely you'll probably be to opt for the choices that are the cheapest and the healthiest. And they're not only the choices that cost the least in the short term but the same ones that save you the most in the long run.

When it comes to long-term savings, there's no better investment you can have than your own robust health. Maintaining good physical and mental health saves you big bucks on health care and other insurance costs over the course of your lifetime. Even if you're lucky enough to be covered by an employer-paid health care plan, you're probably subject to deductibles, copays, and costs for conditions and procedures not in your plan. Other types of insurance, including life, disability, and catastrophic illness, also take into account your health history when determining premiums. And because automobile insurance premiums reflect your driving record, they are ultimately influenced by health-related issues like eyesight, physical and mental agility, and use of drugs and alcohol.

Even if you're still young or covered by an employer's health care plan, and insurance costs aren't a concern for you now, later in life they will be. It's better to stay healthy than to try to get healthy when the employer-paid insurance runs out.

But saving on health care and insurance costs is only the tip of the catheter when it comes to the potential to skip some mega Money Steps—and save some serious wampum—in our quest for healthy bodies and sound minds.

Money Step Aerobics

You might have guessed by now that I'm not the kind of guy who belongs to a health club.

In part that's because of the expense, but it's also because I feel awkward and uncomfortable around people who are exercising. There's something too personal, too familiar about it. It gives me flashbacks of Coach Sacstretcher, wearing only his jockstrap, straddling the bench in the boys' locker room while attempting to pinch out a charley horse in his right buttock. He looked like Cro-Magnon Man clumsily trying to pluck a tick off his hairy ass. That's not an image I like to recall, particularly if I have to buy a twelve-hundred-dollar gym membership for the privilege.

As my wife will attest, I lack the vanity gene when it comes to my personal appearance. But I have to say that my inner miser is flattered by the number of people who say that I look in great shape for a man of almost fifty. And on the basis of my latest physical exam, it's true: I weigh almost exactly what I weighed the day I graduated from college, and I have a resting heart rate of just fifty-five beats per minute and a total body fat of about 11 percent.

Having maintained my fitness without a single day of gym membership or purchasing a single piece of specialized fitness equipment (other than my bicycle, which for me is transportation, first and foremost), I can truthfully respond to such compliments by saying, "Gee, it must be all that cheap living." You see, I'm a big advocate of what I call Money Step Aerobics, my program for getting and staying fit by *not* spending money. Not only is Money Step Aerobics the least expensive way of staying fit (it actually makes you money), but it may also well be the most effective plan because it's a lifestyle choice and not a fitness fad or piece of equipment that will quickly bore you.

Here are some typical Money Step Aerobic exercises and their benefits, both physical and fiscal:

Activity	Savings* (per hour)	Calories† (per hour)	Muscles Used**
• Wash your own car	$15	610	B, UA, LL
• Cut your own grass	$40	648	T, B, LL, UA, LA
• Walk instead of taxiing (4 miles)	$8	864	T, B, LL
• Run instead of taxiing (6 miles)	$10	1080	T, B, LL
• Bicycle instead of taxiing (14 miles)	$20	1080	T, B, LL, LA
• Paint your own house	$25	540	B, UA, LA
• Shovel your own snow	$25	648	T, B, LL, UA, LA
• Rake your own leaves	$15	464	T, B, LL, UA, LA, A
• Clean your own house	$20	324	T, B, LL, UA, LA
• Do your own gardening	$20	486	B, UA, LA
• Clean your own gutters	$20	540	B, UA, LA
• Cut your own firewood	$25	648	B, UA, LA

*Estimated savings are for only one hour of labor costs.

†Calories burned are based on a 180-pound person performing the activity for one hour. To customize for your weight and activities, see www.primusweb.com/fitnesspartner/jumpsite/calculat.htm.

**Muscle group abbreviations: B—back; T—thighs; LL—lower legs: UA—upper arms / shoulders; LA—lower arms; A—abdominals.

Put the Work Back in Workout, as Nature Intended

Money Step Aerobics and the Amazing Cheapskate Diet, which I'll talk about in a minute, are based on the simple premise that if humans do what they are meant to do and eat what they are meant to eat, they will have optimal health. Notice I said "optimal" (i.e., the best something can be in a given situation), not "perfect" or even "good"; injuries and illnesses are facts of life and inevitably facts of death.

So why don't more people do what they were meant to do and eat what they were meant to eat? In large part it's because of—you guessed it—money. Sadly, in much of the world a lack of money and the resources it can buy leads to malnutrition, unhealthy living and working conditions, and premature death (see page 96). But in America it's more commonly the opposite side of the money equation—too much money, not too little— that poses a health risk; more specifically, it's our quest to get and spend more money that's the problem.

When it comes to exercise, humans, like all animals, should get the amount they need just through the normal course of living. Humans are of course the only animals that exercise just for the sake of exercising, because we are the only animals that have so dramatically altered our "normal course of living" and our diets that we need to engage in extracurricular exercise. Well, that's not entirely true. In recent human history we've not been content just to ruin our own health; we've also disrupted food chains, damaged the environment, and, in the case of domesticated animals, deliberately altered the diets and lifestyles of various other species to the point where they too could benefit from a fifty-dollar-an-hour spinning class.

Dietitians tell us that a healthy human diet consists of about 2,000 to 2,500 calories consumed daily. If you think about humans living the type of seminomadic, hunting / gathering lifestyle they were originally intended to live, those calories were typically expended in performing a range of daily activities, including walking, running, lifting, bending, climbing, and pulling. Walking and standing for eight hours a day alone burn about 2,650 calories, as opposed to sitting at a desk for the same eight hours, which burns only about 1,300 calories.

Again, if we allow for some environmental and cultural exceptions, it's clear that performing these daily activities resulted in optimal fitness, burning the amount of fuel we were intended to put in our bodies. In addition, in today's language, these lifestyle activities worked every muscle group; otherwise we wouldn't have evolved those muscle groups in the first place.

As you can see from my list of Money Step Aerobic exercises, I'm not proposing that we all return to a hunting / gathering lifestyle, as much as I occasionally enjoy donning my loincloth and picking wild grapes on a warm late-summer day. But there is an alternative choice that makes sense: Stop paying other people to do so many things for you, and you can then stop spending money on fitness equipment and programs that you don't need. Do more things for yourself, and get your exercise naturally.

One last word about Money Step Aerobics and getting your exercise the way nature intended. The best New Year's resolution I ever made was a few years ago, when I vowed to spend at least one solid hour outdoors in the elements—sun or rain, cold or hot—every single day. Like most people, I realized that my life had devolved to the point where I was, for all intents and purposes, an indoor creature. I inhabited a man-made, climate-controlled environment to the near-total exclusion of the one nature intended.

So whether it's sitting outside for an hour every day reading, writing, or eating my lunch, or, more commonly, getting some exercise and saving some money by performing one of the outdoor Money Step Aerobic activities listed earlier, I'm at least making an effort to return myself to my native habitat, the great outdoors. (Hey, perhaps I can get a grant from the World Wildlife Fund or PETA; you know, "For pennies a day, you can return this cheapskate to his native environment.")

This simple resolution has had a profound impact on both the quality of my life and my health. I've experienced all the health benefits the medical community attributes to spending time outdoors in the fresh air, from fewer respiratory colds to healthier skin, a more positive mental attitude, and a trimmer waistline, since exercising outdoors in variable temperatures burns more calories than the same exercise performed in a climate-controlled environment.

If only health spas could find a way to simulate fresh air, natural sunlight, and being outdoors, they could make a fortune selling such a treatment. But until then I guess we'll just have to get it for free.

Amazing Cheapskate Diet Transfers Weight from Thighs to Wallet

Near the top of my Top Ten Stupid Need More Money Myths list has to be the statement I've heard repeatedly from both fitness "experts" and everyday people: "It costs more to eat healthy." What flummadiddle. If you believe that, you should have the U.S. Department of Agriculture's Food Pyramid surgically attached to your butt so that it reminds you every time you sit down to a meal just how wrong you are.

Once again, the ironic reality is that the *less* money you spend on food—the *right* food—the healthier your diet is likely to be. Conversely, if you spend lavishly on food, chances are your diet will be vastly inferior to one at the opposite end of the cost spectrum. It will almost certainly be inferior from a nutritional perspective, and believe it or not, it may be inferior in terms of taste and enjoyment as well.

To prove my point, start by looking at the USDA Food Pyramid, as difficult as that might be for those of you wearing it on your ass. Although this bellwether of nutritional wisdom has undergone a makeover in recent years (it now looks a little like a Masonic logo designed by Timothy Leary; see www

.MyPyramid.gov), its basic recommendations for a sound diet remain mostly unchanged.

At the base of the pyramid (i.e., those things you should eat the most) are whole grains, bread, cereal, rice, and pasta, although white rice and pasta have moved higher on the revamped pyramid. The next layer is fruits and vegetables, on top of which are nuts and legumes, topped by fish, poultry, and eggs. At the very top of the pyramid—those things that should be the smallest portion of your diet—are red meats, dairy products, sweets, and processed foods containing saturated and trans fat.

Now for the really good news: With a few exceptions, if you look at what these different types of foods typically cost, you'll see that a food *cost* pyramid would be the exact inverse of the dietary food pyramid. In other words, the foods you should be eating most often (like grains, fruits, and vegetables) tend to cost the least. It's the expensive stuff—like red meats, cheeses, and processed foods—that's bad for you, particularly if you can afford to eat them in large quantities. That's proof positive that if there is an intelligent designer at work in our universe, he's definitely a cheapskate!

Of course what most Americans actually shovel down their throats every day bears little resemblance to what the U.S. Department of Agriculture tells us we should eat. With nearly 45 percent of all Americans considered overweight (a full 20 percent of them are classified as obese) our actual diet in many cases is pretty much the exact opposite of the one recommended by the USDA. Alas, if we could only afford to spend less on food, we'd eat so much better.

Compared with most people of the world, Americans (even at the lowest economic levels) have wealth that permits the luxury of eating higher on the food pyramid—and in essence higher on the food chain—than their health can afford. We compensate with our superior (and expensive) health care system and our endless (and expensive) fad diets and exercise plans. Yet again we find ourselves marching down the Money Steps, flight after flight:

Earn money
> **Spend it on expensive, unhealthy food**
>> **Earn more money to spend on repairing poor health, because of expensive food**

(Repeat)

From a dietary standpoint, as evidenced by our world-class waistlines and resulting maladies like diabetes, heart disease, and high blood pressure, we are among the most nutritionally impoverished people in the developed world because of our wealth. What's the answer? Gee, maybe, *spend less* in order to eat healthier?

World Hunger Stinks
(But It Doesn't Have To)

He read in the paper that it only takes ten dollars a year to feed a kid in India, so he sent his kids there.   Red Buttons

If you don't laugh, it's too easy to cry when you start digging into the sad reality of world hunger. A few depressing facts, but then some good news, so hang on:

- Worldwide 1 in 12 people, including 160 million children under the age of five is clinically malnourished.
- Approximately one-third of the world is well fed, one-third

is underfed, and one-third is starving, according to the World Health Organization.

- In the United States 1 out of every 8 children under the age of twelve goes to bed hungry every night, and 1 out of every 6 elderly people has an inadequate diet.
- Every 3.6 seconds someone in the world dies of hunger. That's about 10 people just in the time it's taken you to read this far on this page.

"I know, I know, I know," you're probably saying to yourself. "It's an awful situation, a huge problem. It's such a huge problem there's no easy solution. In fact, I'm not sure if there even is a solution."

Well, now for the good news. While emphatic about the severity of the problem, experts contend that feeding the world's hungry is just a matter of money. And not that much money either.

In fact you might say the solution to world hunger is right under our noses. According to the Web site www.globalissues.org, it would cost about thirteen billion dollars annually to satisfy the world's basic sanitation and food requirements. Where can we free up that kind of cash? Perfume.

That's right, the world's hungry could be fed for about what Americans and Europeans spend on perfume each year. I say, "Chuck the Chanel and feed the children instead!"

Think about that the next time you're tempted to splurge on a fragrance, and instead send a donation to a qualified nonprofit organization that's working to end world hunger. Find qualified charities at www.GuideStar.org or www.charitywatch.org, or consider supporting one of these fine groups:

- **Action Against Hunger** (www.actionagainsthunger.org): Provides hunger relief programs in more than forty countries, specializing in emergency situations like wars and natural disasters.

- **America's Second Harvest** (www.secondharvest.org): America's Food Bank Network, collecting and distributing nearly two billion pounds of food and grocery products each year to those who need it in the United States.
- **Bread for the World** (www.bread.org): A nationwide Christian movement that seeks justice for the world's hungry people by lobbying U.S. decision makers.
- **Freedom from Hunger** (www.freedomfromhunger.org): International development organization that focuses on fostering sustainable self-help solutions in fourteen countries.
- **Global Hunger Project** (www.thp.org): Programs in Africa, Asia, and Latin America that incorporate sustainable strategies for ending hunger and poverty, particularly by empowering women in those regions.

Wouldn't the world smell a lot better to you if we skipped the perfume and solved the problem of world hunger instead?

Under a Dollar a Pound, Year-Round

Saving money on the family grocery bill has become a trophy sport among cheapskates. I guess that's because food is the one commodity that nearly everyone has to buy, so the grocery store is the Superdome when it comes to flaunting your thrift-craft.

In fact there's an entire sect of cheapskates—Couponeers—who are dedicated almost exclusively to competitive grocery shopping. You've seen one in the grocery store before. The typical Couponeer is a slacks-clad woman, age thirty to fifty-five, with a pregnant-looking envelope full of coupons tucked securely in her grocery cart and on a string around her neck a pair of schoolkid scissors (her weapon of choice for spur-of-the-moment in-store clipping). On double-coupon days Couponeers are out in force. On rare triple-coupon days they can be downright dangerous.

I'm not much of a Couponeer myself, in part because most coupons steer you toward brand-name products that, even after the coupon discount, usually cost more than comparable nonbrand-name products when they're on sale. The other reason why I stay away from couponing is that I've always been nervous around large groups of excited, scissor-wielding women. It's kind of a Bobbitt Complex, I guess.

My own approach to grocery shopping is simple: I shy away from buying *anything* that costs more than one dollar a pound. Based as much on the nutritional issues discussed above as on saving money (and, of course, strutting my thrifty ass in front of the Couponeers), this simple rule strikes most people as simple, as in "simply impossible." But take a closer look.

- **Remember your base.** The base of the food pyramid, that is. Obviously there's no innate correlation between a pound of foodstuff and its nutritional or health value; a pound of diet soda has no calories and no real nutritional value, a pound of peanut butter has about 2,600 calories (1,800 of those from fat), and a pound of carrots has about 150 calories, with hardly any fat. But I find that the under-a-dollar-a-pound rule not only helps you keep the relative costs of different foods in perspective but helps steer you toward good nutritional choices because of the inverted food cost pyramid I mentioned before. Even a novice economizer should be able to find most of the things we should be eating the most of, like whole grains (e.g., barley, bulgur, corn, oats, whole grain rice, wheat; see www.wholegrainscouncil

.org), breads, cereal, rice, pasta, for under one dollar a pound. So despite the fact that you can spend a dollar a pound for foods that have no nutritional value or are even bad for you, the under-one-dollar-a-pound search engine generally points you in the right direction.

- **Pay attention to the three reasons to shop in season.** I claimed earlier that the Amazing Cheapskate Diet will not only save you money and make you healthier but also be tastier than the more expensive fare you're probably eating now. One of the reasons for this claim is that in order to keep it under a dollar a pound, you'll need to eat the freshest, tastiest fruits and vegetables, the ones that are in season—poor you. In most regions of the United States, there's hardly any type of fruit or vegetable that you can't get for under a dollar a pound if you shop carefully and buy in season. So you'll not be eating watermelon in the middle of winter—you'll be enjoying in-season citrus like grapefruits and oranges— but who cares since even the most expensive watermelon tastes lousy when it's not in season? As for cooking staples you need year-round like tomatoes, when they're out of season, try substituting canned tomatoes, which can always be found for less than a dollar a pound.

- **For greater variety, limit yourself to what's on sale.** Confused? I'll bet if you plan your meals around only what's on sale on the front page of the weekly supermarket tabloid (i.e., the best of the best weekly deals—aka cherry-picking), you'll end up enjoying a tastier and more varied menu than if you grocery shop without any limits. Setting parameters on the ingredients you have to work with is truly a mother of invention. You'll find yourself actually *thinking* about what you're going to prepare, not just cooking the same half dozen dishes. You'll find yourself experimenting with different cooking techniques, seasonings, and recipes that you'd never try if your grocery budget was limitless. For example, in our area you can nab chicken leg quarters (leg and thigh portion) for as little as twenty-nine cents a pound if you keep your eyes on the weekly sales and buy them in ten-pound bags. Using those as my foundation, I could probably prepare them one hundred distinctly different ways (don't believe me? See below, for starters), each in a recipe that ends up costing much less than a dollar a pound, even if I add cheese or other pricey ingredients. Cooking Web sites like www.Epicurious.com allow you to search for recipes based on the ingredients you have to work with and other needs (e.g., "kid-friendly," dietary restrictions, prep time).

- *¿Habla Cheapskate?* Because most people of the world can't afford to wreck their health with an American-style diet, honoring the under-a-dollar-a-pound vow can mean dining on exotic, gourmet cuisine from around the globe—tough, I know. It's hard to find a culture that eats as high on the food chain as Americans, so fare from almost any other part of the world stands to be a good deal less expensive—and healthier—than our own. Remember those twenty-nine-cent-a-pound chicken leg quarters? Try circling the globe with them: Hispanic (chicken quarters Veracruz style, with tomatoes, peppers, olives, and rice), Caribbean (chicken quarters jerk style—savory flavor), Southeast Asian (chicken quarters grilled with lemongrass), African (chicken quarters tibs—spicy Ethiopian stew), Indian (chicken quarters Punjab style—in a fiery sauce), Mediterranean (chicken quarters with olives, garlic, and lemon), and

Middle Eastern (chicken quarters with chickpeas and honey). Dishes from these cultures commonly incorporate whole grains and legumes—foodstuff easily scored for under a buck a pound—and use meat as an accent, if at all.

- **Avoid my two pet Ps.** How would you like a job shredding lettuce or peeling carrots for one hundred dollars an hour? Or maybe making frozen lasagnas at almost double that pay rate? That was the gist of a research study I remember reading about a few years ago that looked at the astronomical cost people pay when they buy prepared foods. In other words, when you look at the minimal time involved in peeling your own carrots versus buying them already peeled and the dramatic difference in price, you're paying premium wages for the convenience when you compute it on an hourly basis. Prepared and processed foods, my two pet Ps, are Money Steps you'll be happily forced to avoid by adhering to the under-one-dollar-a-pound rule. Home-cooked, made-from-scratch meals are another sacrifice you'll make by spending less. Many prepared and processed foods, including cookies, crackers, snack foods, and frozen dinners, are also evildoers when it comes to containing saturated and trans fats.

- **Consider the spice of life.** Checking out your host's medicine cabinet is a time-honored tradition among partygoers, but I'm a spice rack peeper myself. I'm always interested to see what spices people keep on hand and test my hypothesis that 98 percent of all those cute little spice bottles hanging on everyone's kitchen wall go unopened until they petrify. I know for a fact that my great-aunt has in her spice rack the original myrrh and frankincense gifted to baby Jesus by the three Wise Men (not to mention a gold crown on her second bicuspid of dubious origins). Given that nearly every American kitchen has one of these unused spice racks, I'm convinced that there are at least seventeen nations around the globe with spice-producing economies that owe their entire livelihoods to the sale of trophy spices to Americans. Rather than just skip this Money Step (i.e., don't buy the spices if you're not going to use them), in this case I say try actually to use the spices and hang something else on your kitchen wall (like maybe that hernia truss I saw in your medicine cabinet). Historically, spices served as an economical way of turning basic, inexpensive ingredients into appetizing fare, with their sometimes high cost per ounce offset by the fact that you use only a pinch at a time. Americans have the economic luxury of using large quantities of fat, salt, and sugar as their primary spices, allowing them to use their other spices for display purposes only. The Amazing Cheapskate Diet will inspire you to break open those little bottles. Better yet, buy spices in bulk for cheap at most ethnic and international food stores, and check the dollar store for basic spices at a great price. Also, try growing a pot or two of fresh herbs; they're easy to grow, and the size of the continuous harvest will surprise you.

• **Milk it for all it's worth:** Don't overdo it, but milk, eggs, yogurt, and other dairy products like sour cream and even cream cheese are easily had for under one dollar a pound. For example, a gallon of milk (at about three dollars) works out to about forty cents a pound, and a dozen large eggs (at about one dollar) cost about sixty-six cents a pound. The USDA says that most people can safely eat at least a couple of servings of these foods each day. We normally think of consuming most dairy products in their basic form (e.g., a glass of milk, a container of yogurt) and mostly for breakfast, and we forget about their potential as the backbone of an entire evening meal. Dairy-based soups and sauces using milk, yogurt, sour cream, and the like turn a skimpy dish into a hearty dinner, and in other countries, from Australia to Zanzibar, the simple egg is transformed into an elegant evening meal.

- **Regard the meat (and cheese) of the matter.** "So you're a vegetarian?" That's the first question I usually get when I espouse my doctrine of under-one-dollar-a-pound. No, in fact I like all types of meat, a lot. I have to admit that it's difficult, and in many cases virtually impossible, to find much red meat, seafood, or cheese that meets my spending requirement. Luckily poultry— at least chicken and turkey—can almost always be had for under one dollar a pound, and you'll recall that those are among the meats most recommended by the USDA. Pork is often an ally as well in my occupation of the DMZ (dollar maximum zone). I'm also fortunate because some of my favorite cuts of red meat happen to be of the offal variety (e.g., heart, liver, kidneys) that can easily be had for less than a buck. Not that I expect most readers to embrace my magnificent organs as a result of reading this, but stop by sometime and I'll broil you a chunk of cow's heart (at fifty-nine cents a pound) that you'll swear is the finest filet mignon you've ever eaten. So, red meat, seafood, and some dairy products (cheese and butter, specifically) are why I qualify my under-one-dollar-a-pound rule with the words "shy away from" as opposed to "never buy." Yes, I occasionally swallow hard and stick a cut of meat or wedge of cheese in my grocery cart that costs more than a dollar a pound, although very rarely more than two to three dollars a pound. But notice the perspective that's emerged thanks to adopting my under-one-dollar-a-pound principle:

The
most
expensive
foods are now the
ones that you're buying
the smallest amounts of and
using to cap off a well-balanced diet,
a diet based on foods costing under one dollar a pound.

✏ EXERCISE: How Can My Butt Be So Big? I Always Take the Money Steps

How much money do you spend each year demolishing your health? How much do you then spend trying to repair it? Can you skip or reduce some of the Money Steps and save both your health and your wealth?

Use the following equations to get the Ultimate Cheapskate's estimate of how much cash you're wasting by taking unnecessary health and fitness Money Steps every year. Don't worry about being too exact with your estimates; just go for it.

HEALTH DEMOLITION COSTS

Unhealthy Meals: Fast food and other unhealthy meal choices. Use the USDA Food Pyramid—www.MyPyramid.gov—to rate your meal choices, and be honest!

——— (A: Average number of unhealthy meals per week)

X ——— (B: Average cost per unhealthy meal)

——— (C: Multiply A times B, and enter subtotal here)

——— (D: Multiply A times 2 [dollars], the Ultimate Cheapskate's ample budget a for healthy meal, and enter the total here)

——— (E: Subtract D from C, and enter subtotal here)

X 52

——— (F1: TOTAL spent on unhealthy meals: Multiply E times 52 [weeks] and enter annual total here)

Unhealthy Snacks: Again, use the USDA Food Pyramid to rate your snacks.

——— (A: Average number of unhealthy snacks per week)

X ——— (B: Average cost per unhealthy snack)

——— (C: Multiply A times B, and enter subtotal here)

——— (D: Multiply A times 25 [cents], the Ultimate Cheapskate's ample budget for a healthy snack, and enter the total here)

——— (E: Subtract D from C, and enter subtotal here)

X 52

——— (F2: TOTAL spent on unhealthy snacks: Multiply E times 52 [weeks], and enter annual total here)

Cigarettes

——— (A: average spent on cigarettes per week)

X 52

——— (B: Multiply A times 52 [weeks], and enter subtotal here)

X 2

——— (C: TOTAL: Multiply B times 2, the Ultimate Cheapskate's guesstimate factor of how much more smoking costs you in nonfatal illnesses, lost productivity, etc., and enter total here)

Booze

——　(A: Average spent on alcohol per week)

X 52

——　(B: Multiply A times 52 [weeks], and enter subtotal here)

-$365

——　(C: TOTAL: Subtract $365, the Ultimate Cheapskate's estimate of
what the USDA-recommended one or two glasses of wine per day
should cost you per year, and enter the total or 0 here,
whichever is greater)

Avoiding Activity

Use the list of activities on page 91 (plus any others that apply to you;
see www.primusweb.com/fitnesspartner/jumpsite/calculat.htm) to estimate how much you spend each year paying other people to do things
you want to avoid doing yourself and burning calories you could be
burning.

Cost Annually	Activity	Calories You Paid Someone Else to Burn for You
$ _____	_____	_____
$ _____	_____	_____
$ _____	_____	_____
$ _____	_____	_____
$ _____	_____	_____

TOTAL $ _____

HEALTH REPAIR COSTS

Estimate the total amount you spend each year on the following:

- Fitness club membership $ _____
- Exercise equipment $ _____
- Personal trainer $ _____
- Special diet programs, books, etc. $ _____
- Lost wages because of ill health $ _____
- Out-of-pocket medical expenses for preventable conditions $ _____

TOTAL $ _____

Add together your Health Demolition Costs and your Health Repair Costs to determine the size of your annual health / fitness Money Step. What's your body type?

— **La-Z-Boy Recliner:** Fat Butt / Thin Wallet
— **Fashionable Fit (aka 24/7 Money Step Climber):** Small Butt / Thin Wallet
— **Cheapskate Physique:** Small Butt / Fat Wallet

When Your Cupboard's Stripped Bare

The other day my wife found my cache, a thick roll of one-dollar bills neatly bound with a rubber band (actually, a bright blue rubber band recycled off a bunch of broccoli) and tucked away in my sock drawer.

"So, you said you were going to do some *research* today? If your research involves this roll of dollars and an afternoon at Bambi's Body Shop, don't bother coming home tonight!" Denise warned.

"Honey, you know me better than that. I have standards, you know," I said, reassuring her that I wasn't planning a visit to Bambi's, Southern Maryland's Premiere [sic] Gentleman's Club. "I could never bring myself to spend that kind of money."

Denise just rolled her eyes. A devoted husband? Sure. A devoted cheapskate? Absolutely. I stuffed the roll of greenbacks in my pocket and headed out for some really hot action, an afternoon at the dollar store.

With the twenty-five singles I'd been squirreling away, I wanted to see what cheapskate essentials I could stock an empty kitchen pantry with, assuming that the cupboard's as bare as Bambi's back-side. I'd limit my shopping to the local dollar store, where everything is a dollar, except for some two-for-one-dollar items noted below. I was looking for bargain basics, nonperishable items that should be in every frugal chef's kitchen at all times, not ingredients for a complete meal(s). These are the catalysts of cheapskate cuisine.

Here's how I spent my Michigan bankroll:

1. Canned tomatoes (two sixteen-ounce cans for one dollar): *the* cheapskate kitchen essential. Healthy, cheap, keeps forever. Salads, salsas, sauces, soups, stews—and those are only a few of the *S* possibilities.

2. Bouillon cubes: Chicken, beef, or vegetable—your choice, but they're all similar in flavor. Yes, vastly inferior to homemade stock or even the canned stuff, but for pennies and in seconds you can transform the most meager leftover scraps into a tasty cup of soup. More than once I've turned back while en route to my compost pile, deciding instead to cook up the veggie scraps with a bouillon cube for lunch.

3. Olive oil: I buy it by the gallon and rarely use anything else, but for a buck I'll keep the twelve-ounce bottle on hand for emergencies.

4. Vinegar: Vinegar, it's not just for salads anymore. From poaching eggs to freshening air, from removing chewing gum to reducing static cling, from cleaning windows to scrubbing toilets, vinegar is your friend when you're in a pickle (or if you're a pickle). See www.frugalliving.about.com/cs/tips/a/vinegar.htm for more tales and tips from the sour side.

5. Balsamic vinegar: The older brother white vinegar always wished it had: cool, powerful, and nothing like the rest of the family. Use it as you would regular vinegar (only more sparingly), then cut loose by making a reduction (aka "boilin' it down") to use on everything from meat to ice cream. Downside: You can't clean your toilet with it (I think).

6. Sea salt: I usually stick with kosher salt—less expensive and usually just as good—but heck, for a buck I was curious what beach the dollar store harvests its bargain-priced sea salt from. Distinctive Coppertone flavor.

7. Peppercorns: Never, ever buy the preground stuff, especially when you can get the real thing for less. If you grew up on ground black pepper, welcome to a bold new world.

8. Rice: The USDA says beware of how much of the white stuff you eat, and I trust its science, but I'm struck by the typical body type of the billions of people around the globe who eat white rice as a staple. Too many Americans look as if they have a couple of those fit folks strapped around their waist. Don't overdo it, but I say roll the dice and eat the rice, particularly in soups and casseroles, where it's used in moderation.

9. Pasta (two sixteen-ounce packages for a dollar): See above comments on white rice. The USDA has also cooled on pasta as a staple, at least the non–whole grain variety,

and remember the sizable shadow cast by Brando's pasta-addicted Godfather. But there are plenty of worse choices, including almost anything at a fast-food restaurant.

10. Vanilla extract: A big bottle of the cheap imitation stuff is fine for the liberal uses I have in store—flavoring fruit smoothies, sprinkling on desserts, adding to salad dressings, for example.

11. Cinnamon: Not just a dessert-making staple, but borrow a page from Indian and Middle Eastern chefs, and use it to add that distinctive, savory flavor to meat and vegetable dishes as well.

12. Italian seasoning: The catchall spice mix, because it contains most of the spice super stars—oregano, basil, thyme, marjoram. Add to O & V to dress a salad, sprinkle on meat, poultry, and seafood before grilling, or use to flavor soup stock and other recipes in a pinch.

13. Canned jalapeño peppers: OK, a bit of a personal choice, but I always want to have something on hand that has incredible potency and versatility. Chop up these green devils to add punch and depth to just about any casserole, soup, or other cooked dish, or mix with cream cheese for a spicy app. Don't like spicy food? Just don't put so much in.

14. Bread crumbs: Sure, use your stale bread to make your own, but keep some on hand as a healthier alternative to flour when breading meats for under the broiler, thickening liquids, or making a light stuffing.

15. Olives: In America they're a nonvoting member of the relish plate; in the Mediterranean and other parts of the world they're a reason for living—literally and figuratively. Use them in salads, sauces, and spreads. The noble olive should be relished, not relish.

16. Lentils: Another perfect food—healthy, delicious, and

cheap. And unlike dried beans, you don't need to soak dried lentils ahead of time. Soup's the obvious choice, but also try them puréed, as a dip or sandwich spread, as a side vegetable, or in a cold salad. Lentils are a natural canvas for showing off other flavors, like vinegar or hot or savory spices.

17. Pickled red peppers: Another pick reflecting some personal bias, but these gems are underappreciated by most Americans. Mild almost to the point of being bland, they add color and a subtle, smoky quality in a hurry to sauces, soups, salads. A cheap way of making a simple dish look and taste richer.

18. Beans (two sixteen-ounce cans or bags of dried beans for one dollar): The dried ones equal more like three or four pounds when soaked and cooked, so you know what I say: "If you don't have enough time to soak your own beans, it's time to take a good look at your life. You're the one getting soaked."

19. Canned fish: Tuna, sardines, or salmon, your choice, two cans for a dollar. Keep an assortment on hand for tasty sandwiches, salads, and appetizers, not to mention a fair share of healthy omega-3 fatty acids.

20. Nuts: At a dollar a bag (four to twelve ounces, depending on type), nuts are a real dollar store value. Stock up on your favorites. Good for your health and easily incorporated into every course of a meal, from soup to, well, nuts.

21. Sunflower seeds: Perfect healthy snack, and don't forget to add them for crunch factor to salads and baked goods.

22. Honey: Nectar of the Cheapskates. On toast it's breakfast; on yogurt it's dessert; in a cup of tea it's "good night all." Think twice whenever you reach for plain sugar.

23. Oatmeal: The good old-fashioned slow-cooking kind—you

know, the kind that takes all of five minutes to prepare.
Don't think just breakfast; use it in cookies, bread, baked
desserts, and even soups and other entrées (see
www.hamlynsoats.co.uk).

24. Baking soda: I am honor-bound by the oath I took to the
    Knights of the Cheaphood to pay homage to baking soda
    at some point in this book. Although it's not a food
    product per se, it is perhaps the most versatile substance
    known to man, particularly cheap man. Few know its
    primary purpose (as an additive in making glass), but
    everyone has an alternative use, or ten. Other cheapskates
    who came before have spoken so thoroughly and
    eloquently, I defer to them on the topic: Read the
    definitive *Baking Soda Book: Resourceful and Ingenious
    Uses of Baking Soda* (by George "TipKing" Hughes) free
    online at www.bakingsodabook.co.uk. Every time my wife
    bemoans being married to the Ultimate Cheapskate, I
    remind her that she could have chosen a man who
    devoted his entire life to baking soda.

My cart was full, and I still had a single dollar left in my roll. I
was thinking about Denise finding my cache that morning and
questioning my motives. I stealthily slipped a one-dollar pink thong
in Denise's size into my shopping cart, one with the subtle message
"YES!!!" spelled out in purple sequins on the crotch. God, I love
the dollar store.

5

Buy a Home, Not a Castle

*In our grandparents' generation you paid off your house
in four or five years, and you stayed married forty or fifty
years. Now those statistics are just about the opposite.*

—the Ultimate Cheapskate

*He always wants to make love a lot more often during
the wintertime. I finally realized that it gives him an
excuse to turn down the thermostat.*

—Denise Yeager commenting on the Ultimate Cheapskate's
thermostatically controlled libido

First-time visitors to our home inevitably have a similar response: "Gee, this is *really* nice!" The assumption is that since I am the Ultimate Cheapskate, my wife and I must live in a roadside Dumpster somewhere or at best in a rusting mobile home.

Now, that's not to say that the House of Yeager is a typical house. Construction started in the 1930s, and my latest estimate is that it will be completed in 2020, although recently that deadline seems optimistic. We have, in all honesty, done all—and I mean *all*—the remodeling ourselves, having started with an interesting, although not particularly well-built house that originally belonged to a Depression-era artist and her husband.

People often comment that the house has a Frank Lloyd Wright feel to it. Certainly during heavy rains there is an impressive Falling Waters–like feature in the middle of the living room, which I catch in a big bucket I keep stored nearby for that purpose.

Much of the house was originally built from recycled materials, like the conversation-starting round glass picture windows salvaged from a federal government building that was torn down during the Depression. We've continued that tradition, incorporating recycled, reclaimed, and readapted building materials and furnishings whenever possible.

This has easily saved us tens of thousands of dollars over the years, and it's given us a truly one-of-a-kind home and something we're extremely proud of, not because of how much it cost, but because of how little it cost and how much it reflects our personalities and interests. It's also given us a chance to share some quality Dumpster-diving and curb-shopping time together, me sporting my favorite Ultimate Cheapskate T-shirt for such occasions: "*Carpe Crape* [pronounced Carp-ay Crap-ay]: Seize the Crap!"

We've indulged our interests in gardening and nature by converting a leaky old in-ground swimming pool into a sunken Japanese water garden, all done using found materials and successfully enough that it was once featured in the *Washington Post*. We recently finished remodeling our kitchen (a two-year project), and the design for the drop ceiling was something I'd sketched years before on a napkin from a bar in the Reykjavik (Iceland) Airport that had a similar one. Of course our built-in wine rack is also a little unusual, designed to accommodate five-liter boxes of wine rather than old-fashioned bottles, which are so last century.

I work from home, or, rather, from garage, having built my small but comfortable office in a corner of our otherwise cluttered garage. I was able to build the entire office out of scrap material that was already in the garage. I also sold unwanted items stored there in order to finance other construction costs. I did splurge on a round burnt orange chair from the 1970s that cost me twenty-five dollars at a local thrift store. It too is a real conversation starter and the perfect "thinking chair" for my office. As I like to say, "If this chair could talk, I'm pretty sure it would either moan or speak only while inhaling."

It's truly an eclectic house, and I don't think we could be happy living in one that wasn't. With each remodeling project we've taken on, we've made it that much more our own, more a reflection of our personalities, tastes, interests, and needs.

In other words, we've done everything real estate agents tell you *not* to do in order to maximize the resale value of your home. God forbid that your home isn't just like everyone else's; otherwise no one will want to buy it! But then again, ours isn't for sale.

We live in a sort of oddball neighborhood of older, owner-built houses, which has fortunately kept its character despite ever-encroaching subdivisions of new GPS homes, minimansions that require GPS to locate all the rooms. But if our home is unique, it fits right in with those of our closest neighbors, all of whom share a similar desire to have their homes express their individuality. In fact ours is pretty tame in that context.

One of our neighbors has two great passions in life: square dancing and playing the alpine horn—you know, those ten-foot-long phalliclike instruments that guys in lederhosen blow in the Swiss Alps. He built his entire house around those two interests, including a regulation-size square dancing hall and several very long, very narrow, windowless rooms with perfect acoustics for the alpine horn.

I told a real estate agent friend about it, and he said, "What an idiot! He'll never in a million years find anyone who will buy that house when he wants to sell!" But I'm not so sure about that. The good news is that when he gets ready to sell, he can really target his potential market. Sure, how many square-dancing alpine hornists can there be, even in a large metropolitan area like Washington, D.C.? But once he finds even one, I think his house will truly sell itself!

Keep the Dream from Becoming a Nightmare

As you probably already know, your house, if you choose to buy one, will almost certainly be the single largest purchase you make in your lifetime. The traditional rule of thumb used by mortgage bankers was that no more than 30 percent of your household income should be spent on housing. But according to the U.S. Department of Housing and Urban Development, housing costs now consume 50 percent or more of the incomes of more than twelve million American families. Even if you don't buy one, housing is still likely to be the single most expensive commodity you'll pay for over the course of your life.

I'm all in favor of striving to achieve the *original* American dream of homeownership. Experts will tell you that Americans who buy homes amass an average of thirty to forty times more wealth over their lifetimes than people who don't. Interpreting that statistic strikes me as a little tricky, as clearly homeownership is both a cause and an effect of wealth—that is, wealthier people are in a better position to buy a house in the first place, and buying a house in turn usually generates more wealth through appreciation. Regardless of interpretation, however, few, if any, financial pundits advise against trying to buy rather than rent housing, and I wholeheartedly agree with that.

But if owning your own home was the original American

dream, today the *new* American dream is to own (excuse me, pay interest toward) your own *castle*. It's this new American dream that I rail against.

Between 1950 and 1993 the average size of a new house built in the United States increased by nearly 90 percent (1,100 versus 2,060 square feet). That's a big jump, but even bigger when you factor in the decreasing household / family size during that same period. In 1950 it was one American per 312 square feet of residential space, but that increased by about 140 percent to 742 square feet by 1993. And it looks as if the trend of supersizing the family homestead is continuing with no end in sight.

Younger generations today often complain that they'll never be able to afford to buy a house, that home prices are just too high. But when you factor in inflation ($1 in 1950 was equivalent to $7.75 in 2005), that 1,100-square-foot house that cost about $14,400 in 1950 would have cost $112,375 in 2005. That's probably not far off what the actual figures would have been and certainly not reflective of any extraordinary increase in housing costs compared with other costs, outside of normal inflation.

But what has changed is our desire for more, for a bigger house. In 2005 the median cost of an average new home—a 2,000-plus-square-foot castle—was actually around $240,000, roughly double in price and double in size of the back-of-the-envelope example given above. It looks to me as if it's our appetites, not housing prices, that have shot up so dramatically in recent years.

So we want to own a castle, not just a house as our grandparents did. Well, on second thought, maybe "own" is the wrong word. According to "The Illusion of Home Ownership," an article published on the Web site www.blueridgemuse.com, "fewer than 10% of Americans will pay off a home mortgage, down from 44% just 25 years ago."

I'm sure that trend is attributable to a number of things, not the least of which is the fact that many financial pundits advise against paying off your mortgage, at least any earlier than you need to. That's a myth I'll address in just a minute. But here's a simple observation: Could it also be due to the fact that we're spending more than we can afford, both on our castles and on other things that we leverage our homes to buy?

Home Economics

Talk about homesickness! Think about these sad stats as you're falling asleep tonight in your cozy casa:

- *Can crazy:* Americans spend approximately ten billion dollars a year remodeling their bathrooms. In 1973, 40 percent of new homes had fewer than two bathrooms; by 2005, 95 percent of new homes had two or more bathrooms, and 26 percent had three or more bathrooms. Note that 40 percent of the world's population does not have indoor plumbing.
- *Culinary contradictions:* Since the 1950s the average size of a kitchen in a new American home has more than tripled, to approximately 285 square feet. The question is, Who's cooking in those big new kitchens? Between 1980 and 2000 alone, the frequency of purchasing meals outside the home (in restaurants and carryout) more than doubled, to more than 30 percent of all meals we eat. In fact 19 percent of all meals eaten by adults in America are now consumed in automobiles.
- *Three cars in every garage:* Well, I guess if we're dining so often in our cars, it only stands to reason that we have

to have more of them. Of new American homes, 84 percent now come with garages capable of holding more than two cars, more than a 100 percent increase since the 1970s. During the same period, the fuel economy of U.S. automobiles also improved by almost 100 percent. One step forward, two steps back.

- *Leave me alone:* As the American family gets smaller (3.14 persons per household in 1970 down to 2.57 by 2003), the number of bedrooms continues to grow. Of new homes in the United States, 39 percent now have four or more bedrooms. Ironically (or maybe not), during that continuing boudoir growth trend, reported incidents of childhood depression, including thoughts of feeling lonely, isolated, and even suicidal, have increased more than fourfold. (I wanted my own bedroom when I was growing up, but it wasn't to be. I always had to share one with my omni-annoying older brother. Maybe my brother wasn't such bad company after all.)

A Different Approach

As I said earlier, my wife and I live in a home that we love and that is gushingly admired by nearly everyone who ever visits. It's the only house we've ever owned and is likely to be the only one we ever will own.

We bought it in 1986, having rented an apartment for three years after we were first married while we saved up money for a down payment. The house cost $157,000, which was at the outer limit of what we could afford at that time, but we decided to stretch because we were convinced that the house had the potential to be one in which we could be happy, forever.

Now, twenty years later, we're convinced more than ever that it was one of the best financial and lifestyle decisions we ever made. That's not just because like virtually every other home in the United States, our property has appreciated significantly in value. Rather, our joy in homeownership has been increased immeasurably by the fact that we bought a home that was well within our financial means in the long run and that we could, with our own hands, shape into whatever we want it to be.

This peace of mind and the ability to express our individuality through our home have given us value far in excess of the tripling of our initial investment. Our approach to homeownership differs from the current American model in several important ways:

- We bought an older house, one in need of repair but one that had, at least in our eyes, incredible potential to become "our home" and allow us the luxury of expressing our interests and tastes.
- We bought a house that was considered a starter home (albeit a higher-priced one) for a young professional couple like us at that time, but we did so expecting to finish in that starter home.
- We bought a house that as our earnings increased over the years, we could easily afford to pay off early and that also had some income-producing potential via an attached rental unit.
- And we bought a reasonably sized house (approximately 1,800 square feet, including a rental unit and detached home office space), not a castle.

Housing is the Big Kahuna of lifetime spending. How about spending a little less time reassuring ourselves that we can put our financial house in order by giving up our daily cup of Starbucks and thinking for a minute about the housing choices we make?

Finishing in a Starter Home

I have a really radical idea, but one that your grandparents probably wouldn't have raised an eyebrow over: What if you bought a nice starter home when you were young and just stayed there? Or for that matter, if you're no longer all that young, what if you moved to a starter home today?

A couple of generations ago there was no such thing as a starter home. There were just homes, and for the most part you bought one you liked and were happy—indeed most content— to stay there throughout much or all of your life.

If you planned on having children, you took that into account by choosing a house that could expand and contract with your changing family size. That usually meant an extra bedroom or two, not a suite of private rooms for each child, as it commonly does these days (see page 120). When the kids finally left home, mom and dad were rewarded with a couple of hundred square feet of additional living space to spread out in, not an empty warehouse of a house that needed to be put on the market the next day.

A couple of generations ago moving was usually considered a bad thing, a necessary evil, a traumatic uprooting. You moved if your family needed to relocate for a job or, later in life, if you were unable to maintain your family home. But the idea of house climbing, continually trading up to ever larger, more expensive houses, was something most of our grandparents never thought about, let alone engaged in.

If "starter home" were part of a word association test, I should instantly spout out "first marriage" in response. Both terms were initiated by my generation and use adjectives to confer temporary status to things that were previously assumed to be permanent. Both reflect a major shift in my generation's thinking and expectations. Both, in my opinion, have also significantly contributed to my generation's deficit, and I'm not just talking about financial deficits.

House climbers will no doubt flip out when they hear about my radical proposal for finishing in your starter home. How can anyone be content staying in the same house he or she starts out in? Families change, needs change, houses change; you have to change with the times. Don't you? Most of all, given the recent real estate market, what about the tremendous wealth to be built by trading up to increasingly more valuable homes?

Even though I personally place a high value on having a nice house (i.e., one that satisfies *you*), and I'm all in favor of building wealth through buying a home rather than renting one, I think America's current real estate orgy is just that: exciting, and you're likely to get screwed.

At best, the recent real estate boom and the house-climbing trend it has sparked are yet another way for people to chase after wealth they probably don't really need. At worst, it's a disastrous financial decision and diminishes your overall enjoyment of life. We'll come back to all that in a minute.

Feeling Right at Home: Less Is More

In her best-selling book *The Not So Big House*, the author, architect, and interior designer Sarah Susanka makes the compelling case that humans are actually most comfortable living in spaces that are, at least by today's standards, relatively small. Homes of one thousand to fifteen hundred square feet, depending on family size and other factors, are ideal for most people. Once we move in, today's newly built five-thousand-square-foot GPS houses leave us feeling lonely, depressed, uncomfortable, and cold.

I trust and appreciate Susanka's observations from an organic architecture point of view, even though she goes on to argue that a not-so-big house may well cost as much as or more than a big house. She says that's because people value quality—of both materials and design—more than quantity. Because of that, Susanka says the cost per square foot of one of her not-so-big houses will be significantly higher (perhaps 50 percent higher) than the cost per square foot for a lesser-quality GPS home. But then remember, she's in the business of selling architectural and interior design services.

While I can understand that people feel more comfortable working out in a gymnasium than they do living in one, I have to think that some of the feelings of depression and anxiety that come from living in a big house also come from the onus of *paying* for a big house. Also, like so many things that cost a lot of money, once you have it, you don't feel as happy as you thought you would.

If I'm correct, then a not-so-big house with a not-so-big price tag is the best of both worlds. Plus—and it's a big plus—no matter what you pay for your not-so-big house, think of the huge savings you'll be generating on heating, cooling, electricity, maintenance / repair, and even furnishing and decorating over the course of your homeownership.

Susanka's arguments for the superiority of smaller houses should make you take a second look at my idea of finishing in a starter home, particularly one that's older. Not only are older homes generally smaller, but they usually incorporate superior craftsmanship and materials (Susanka's other consideration) and cost less than new construction (the Ultimate Cheapskate's primary consideration). Of course, older homes are often located in more interesting, deeper-rooted communities as well, a tremendous bonus in my opinion.

Making Your House *Your* Home

Best of all, my idea of finishing in a starter home affords you one of life's greatest luxuries, one that most house climbers never get to experience, despite their apparent residential riches. I'm talking about the luxury of being able to make your house your home. By that, I mean having the freedom to redesign, remodel, decorate, customize, and otherwise modify your house around your unique interests, activities, needs, and personalities, without concern for the impact those actions will have on the impending resale of your house.

I'm always struck by the frivolity of those lists you see of the home improvement projects that retain the greatest amount of their value when you go to sell your home. The implication is of course that you'll want to make only those changes that the next guy wants, not necessarily what you want. When will it be your time, time to have a house that is about you, alpine horn practice rooms and all?

For house climbers, the answer is likely to be never, since they're constantly anticipating the next move and sweating over how best to sell the houses they're currently living in. But here's another example of how "settling for less," finishing in a starter home, can actually be more: more satisfying, more comfortable, more rewarding, more enjoyable, and, ironically, more affordable.

Particularly if you're interested in performing some or all of the work yourself (you're definitely capable, as I discuss elsewhere), this transformation of your house into your home can become a lifelong passion. It's as much about an enjoyable hobby as about creating an enjoyable habitat.

You can create and re-create a home that reflects your changing interests, needs, and tastes, and because you are performing the work yourself, you'll be able to redirect and refine those plans even as you work. Financially, if you do the work yourself, many home remodeling and improvement projects can be paid for as you go, per my contention that there is a natural relationship between the amount of work one weekend warrior can perform and that warrior's ability to pay for the required materials.

Even if you've never worked with your hands before or you have little interest in giving it a try, take a few minutes to consider the suggestions in Chapter 8. That's where I make the case that with a little conscious effort you might discover hidden talents and interests you never knew you had. Making your home your hobby may be an acquired taste, but it's a taste well worth acquiring when it comes to saving some major Money Steps in life.

But You Can't Afford *Not* to Get Rich from Real Estate!

Now there's a great title for one of those thousand-dollar-per-person workshops (audiotapes sold separately) that moneymaking late-night infomercial gurus put on every Tuesday evening at your local Holiday Inn Express. I've never attended one of those seminars, so I'll reserve judgment, although as a general life rule I'm always a little suspicious of any proposal that involves one thousand dollars, meeting at a Holiday Inn Express, and some guy wearing a fuchsia patterned Hawaiian shirt. But maybe that's just me.

So can you make a bundle by house climbing, trading up to ever bigger, more expensive homes? If you succeed, you'll indeed have some more wealth, but at what cost in terms of quality of life and happiness? Then there's the downside:

- **But real estate is a *sure thing*.** "It can only go up in value because they're not making any more of it!" How many times have you heard that one? I'm no economist, so I don't know how to evaluate that statement over the long haul, but it's clear that real estate developers are determined to fill our remaining cornfields and neighborhood empty lots with plenty more housing stock. I think that's both unfortunate for our communities and worth considering if you're a house climber. Sure, you own a piece of property with a nice house on it, but you can bet there's a developer down the road plowing under a potato field (redundant?) to build even nicer homes with all the cutting-edge amenities current buyers want. What might that do to your home's value and marketability when the housing market tightens?

- **Living large—in a bubble?** Regardless of long-term real estate values, it's certainly possible to have at least temporary inflation and deflation of real estate values over time. Current real estate values, particularly in certain parts of the country (and even in specific neighborhoods), may well be inflated—perhaps by a lot—creating the much-talked-about bubble prospect. But even if the bubble bursts, and your home suddenly becomes worth much less, what's the big *problema*, you may ask. After all, many types of investment fluctuate in value over time.

If you're a house climber, consider these nightmare scenarios as you're trying to fall asleep tonight:

- **Divorce:** Can you afford to keep up with those monthly payments if you divorce or split with your partner? If not, you'll be forced to sell on the quick, regardless of current market ups or downs, maybe even for less than your outstanding mortgage(s).
- **Home-leveraged debt:** According to economists, America's current negative saving rate is largely driven by the wealth effect attributed to high real estate values. In other words, people are taking on more debt (including home equity loans and credit card debt) because they believe their houses will ultimately make them wealthy. If home values don't continue to support borrowing, the screen doors will slam with foreclosures and bargain sales.
- **Job loss or other emergencies:** If you or your spouse loses a job, can you keep your head above the mortgage tide, including any loans collateralized with the equity in your home? Even if you find another job quickly, it might be in another part of the country and force a distress sale.
- **That's not a house; it's my retirement plan.** This may be, as Fred Sanford use to say on *Sanford and Son,* "the big one" when it comes to perils facing house climbers. More and more Americans are betting the farm on the farm, counting on their homes to appreciate sufficiently in value to fund their retirements. Not only have they

failed to bank other retirement savings, but the only
equity many house climbers have in their homes is the
anticipated increase in their home's value. They've never
lived anywhere long enough to actually make a dent in
the principal amount owned under their mortgages.
Remember that in a typical thirty-year mortgage, only
about 2 percent of the payments you make in the first
year are applied to principal; the rest is all interest. In
the old days, paying down principal, not speculating on
an increase in value, was the way you built equity in
your home.

On this last point, I'm anxious to see what house climbers
have as an endgame when it comes time to cash in the equity
in their GPS homes to fund their retirement.

I suppose the answer will increasingly be reverse mortgages,
although typically when you have a diversified portfolio of
investments, that is considered a source of last resort. Reverse
mortgages are also based on the then current value of your
home (so hope for the best when you need the money) and the
equity you actually have in it after factoring in any outstanding
mortgage amounts and other debt secured by your home. Even
then, you can get a reverse mortgage loan for only a portion of
that balance.

Most house climbers I've talked with say, "We'll sell this
place and buy something less expensive with the equity." OK,
maybe, but I have a hard time seeing many of them happily settling into something less when the time actually comes. After
all, if they could be content with less, why didn't they just stay
in a more modest home in the first place, pay it off, and skip all
the Money Steps in between?

Free at Last: Pay Off Your Mortgage ASAP

If you remember only a couple of pieces of advice from this book, I hope that my recommendations regarding homeownership will be among them. At the top of that list, put my admonition to pay off your #@%$& home mortgage as quickly as possible. For most of us, there is no other financial achievement that guarantees the lifestyle freedom and peace of mind that being mortgage free provides. It truly changes everything and opens opportunities for enjoying life in ways that you've never before even had the luxury of contemplating.

Oddly enough, this onetime benchmark of sound financial management—owning your home free and clear—has in our generation become a sort of antiquated, oft-criticized goal. Many financial planners advise strongly *against* paying off your home mortgage early, generally citing two points to support their position. First is the argument that you will be losing what is likely to be your single largest tax deduction, the interest you pay on your home mortgage. When hearing this, many people somehow think they'll be *losing* money once they no longer have mortgages. Now this is a case of math confusion if I ever saw one! The reality is that for every dollar in mortgage interest you pay, you recover about twenty-eight cents or so (depending on your tax bracket) in tax savings. In other words, you have a net loss of seventy-two cents on every dollar in interest you pay. The financial planner's argument is like saying gambling is a good investment because 28 percent of the time you win your money back.

The second point offered by many financial planners in defense of the "don't pay off your mortgage early" position is that because mortgage loans allow you to borrow money relatively inexpensively, you're better off taking any extra funds you have and investing them rather than prepay your mortgage.

In fact mortgage loans are the cheapest money most people can borrow, not just because of their low interest rates but because of the tax deductibility of the interest, as discussed above. Because of that, you definitely should pay off credit cards and other higher interest rate loans before you attack your home mortgage. You should also contribute the maximum to your 401(k) or other pretax savings plans before prepaying your mortgage, particularly if your employer offers a matching contribution.

But beyond those stipulations, I think you're crazy not to take the sure bet of paying down your mortgage versus the anything but sure bet of investing the money instead. Let's say that on the basis of current mortgage rates and factoring in the net effect of the tax savings described above, your mortgage loan is really costing you only 4 to 5 percent annually. Heck, even CDs pay that much these days, so why shouldn't you take the money and invest it instead?

First, remember, as long you have debt, any money you invest elsewhere is costing you the interest you are paying by not putting that money toward the debt. In this case the money you invest in CDs is costing you the 4 to 5 percent interest you're paying on your home mortgage. When you take that into account, investing in CDs is a break-even proposition at best. But I know you're a savvy investor, so let's say your investments generate a respectable 8 percent annual return. You need to realize that 50 to 62.5 percent of that return (i.e., 4 to 5 percent is 50 to 62.5 percent of a total return of 8 percent) goes just to cover the cost of the money you're "borrowing" to invest with.

That's also before you factor in any taxes or fees associated with those investments, which could easily cut the remainder of your return in half again. Then there's the downside, the very real prospect that your investments might fail to do better than the sure bet of paying down your mortgage.

What's more, in real life even people with the best intentions often fail to actually bank and invest the extra money they decided not to use to pay down their mortgages. It's too easy to decide instead to spend it on something else. With the type of accelerated mortgage plan we used to pay off our mortgage early, you set in motion a sort of forced savings plan, making it easier to resist spending temptations. In fact, by paying off your mortgage early, you *are* investing the money; you're investing it in a piece of real estate that is likely to increase in value.

Even if you have the willpower and invest the money instead, you continue to be a slave to the cash flow demands of making monthly mortgage payments. If you encounter an emergency like a job loss and are unable to make your monthly mortgage payment, you may be forced to liquidate some of your investments in a hurry, perhaps even when they're in a slump. In contrast, if you've paid off your mortgage, your lifestyle options and financial security skyrocket as a result of improved cash flow, once you've eliminated what is typically the single largest monthly demand for cash, your mortgage payment.

What's not to like? A guaranteed rate of return, the financial security and flexibility of improved cash flow, 100 percent ownership of an asset that will probably continue to increase in value, and peace of mind, priceless.

Honey, I Shrank the Mortgage!

If you've ever bought a home, you know there comes a profound moment of reckoning at the closing when the anxious homeowners-to-be review their mortgage documents for the first time. Swear to God, I interrupted the proceedings to point out an obvious typo. But then I realized that a thirty-year mortgage initiated in 1986 would indeed terminate in 2016.

Now, at that time 2016 was the kind of date science fiction writers used as the setting for their futuristic stories of the unimaginable, a world so distant it wasn't even recognizable, not the world in which the Yeager mortgage would finally be paid off. I thought the loan documents should include an escape clause, just in case if by 2016 the world was being ruled by apes or computers or giant women or if by then the Yeagers were merely free-floating, disembodied plasma brains and no longer needed a house.

Between the unfathomable time frames and the staggering dollar amounts involved in purchasing a home today, most people seem to enter a semidelusional state, a sort of debtor dementia, no doubt the body's way of protecting that portion of the human mind that deals with rational thinking. Because of the size and scope of the transaction, the dollars involved seem like play money, and the idea that you'll ever live to see the loan paid off seems like a fairy tale. While it is difficult, you need consciously to counteract this mind-set right from the start, or before long you'll be thinking that a second mortgage or home equity loan is no big deal or that setting the clock back even further by refinancing with a new thirty-year mortgage makes a lot of sense.

In our case we managed to pay off our mortgage long before the world was taken over by giant women (although I sometimes wonder about the influence of computers and apes, at least the kind in elected office). Back in 1986 we took out a thirty-year fixed-rate mortgage when we bought our house because it was the only type of loan we could qualify for at that time, given our incomes and the cost of the house. After five years, as our incomes edged upward and mortgage rates decreased, we were able to refinance and qualify for a fifteen-year fixed rate mortgage on the outstanding balance.

Shortly after that we really put our backs into it and enrolled in a mortgage acceleration program offered by the lender. Most mortgage companies offer similar plans as a relatively painless way of paying off your mortgage early. It requires you to make half a mortgage payment every two weeks (ugh!), *but* the total you pay in a four-week period is the same amount you were previously paying each month. The difference of a few days each month means that the mortgage company gets its money back that much sooner (thereby decreasing total interest charges). You in essence end up making one additional "monthly payment" per year, since you're making twenty-six half payments instead of twelve full monthly payments. That extra payment is hardly noticeable once you get on the biweekly cycle, and you can generally cancel these plans at any time and go back to your monthly schedule if you like.

That mortgage acceleration program and a couple of additional lump sum payments we were able to make late in the game allowed us to retire the fifteen-year mortgage in roughly eleven years. So, in total, we paid off our house in sixteen years as opposed to the unimaginable thirty-year sentence we faced at the beginning.

But where did the extra money come from to meet this more demanding timetable?

- By deciding to finish in a starter home, what was at first an onerous mortgage payment gradually became very manageable as our incomes grew. At that point, rather than follow the path of so many of our peers and "upgrade" to a more expensive house, we doubled down, accelerating the rate at which we were paying off our mortgage, as described above.

- By keeping our eye on the prize—setting a priority on owning our house free and clear ASAP—we avoided the pitfalls encountered by those who suffer from debtor dementia (e.g., second mortgages, home equity loans) that dig you in deeper. As a result, the money we would have been wasting on even more interest payments went instead toward our one and only mortgage.

- We did a good job of locking up any windfalls and periodically applying them as lump sum payments against our mortgage. By "windfalls" I mean relatively small things that most people enjoy from time to time: tax refunds, proceeds from a yard sale, an insurance settlement for a dented bumper we'll never get fixed, a holiday bonus, or a little overtime pay. We set up a special money market account specifically to lock these amounts away until we had enough that it made sense to bother with a lump sum payment.

- Most of all, we followed our own advice for spending less and enjoying life more.

Putting *Neighbors* Back in Our *Neighborhoods*

One final thought on the premise of this chapter, that when it comes to housing, like so many other things, if you're searching for more, you're likely to find it in less.

To that end, think for just a moment about the impact that a simple concept like finishing in your starter home stands to have on our families, communities, and world. Our communities and, as a result, our families suffer when residents don't stick around long enough to put down roots, to come to know and care for their neighbors, to get involved in community institutions and shoulder some of the shared responsibilities that strengthen the social fabric of our nation. And our attitude toward housing as a disposable commodity is both wasting resources and giving us an environment void of sense of place and history.

Only by accepting less can we regain these precious commodities. You don't need to play the alpine horn or have a house designed around one to want more. Or less, as the case may be when it comes to your home.

Houses that Earn a Living: A Beautiful Thing

We love our home, despite its occasional demonic possession. Sometimes I swear it has a mind of its own, one that's determined to make me take my own life by forcing myself, inch by inch, down the kitchen garbage disposal.

Like the time the septic tank backed up just as we were clearing the last dishes from a huge family Thanksgiving dinner. Or the month when cash was really tight and the dishwasher, clothes dryer, and hot-water heater all secretly conspired to stop working on the exact same day. Coincidence? I think not.

But every time I'm ready to call in an exorcist or a real estate agent, I remember one of the very special things about our home: It earns a pretty decent living. I'm not talking about its increasing value as an asset. I'm talking about a home that produces its own cash flow, a home that helps pay for itself.

As I've mentioned, when my wife and I purchased our home in 1986, the house we fell in love with was a real stretch for us financially at that time. But as the real estate agent anxiously pointed out, there was a one-bedroom guest apartment attached to the main house that could be rented out to help cover the ominous monthly mortgage payments.

At first this proposition really turned us off. We had no experience managing a rental property, and we had nightmarish thoughts of ill-mannered tenants destroying our home and sticking us for the rent. We loved the privacy and solitude of our dream house, and we imagined those same qualities being destroyed by boisterous tenants living only a wall away.

Nonetheless, our adoration of this special home got the best of us, and we decided to do whatever was necessary to swing the mortgage payments, including using the guest apartment as a rental property. We reassured ourselves that we would get out of the landlord business the minute our incomes allowed us to cover the mortgage without relying on a monthly rent check.

But more than two decades later, with our house now entirely paid off, we're still happily renting out our little guest apartment and have every intention of continuing to do so forevermore. We have found that rather than being a pox upon our homeownership experience, our rental unit has not only steadily augmented our income but has been a net positive in terms of creating lasting friendships with like-minded tenants who have shared our back wall over the years.

If you're fortunate enough to find a home that will accommodate this type of arrangement, the financial beauty cannot be overstated. First, of course, is the monthly rent check, which in our case covered roughly one-third of our monthly mortgage payment month in and month out. Not bad when you consider that our rental unit is only about 20 percent of the total square footage of the property.

But the financial benefits of such an arrangement don't end with the monthly rent checks. While that rental income is taxable, you can deduct a variety of expenses against that income, including mortgage and other interest expenses associated with the property, depreciation, and a host of maintenance and repair costs. While in most years our taxable income has increased because of this rental property, by keeping careful track of our offsetting expenses, we have kept the year-end tax liability at a minimum.

Most surprising to us have been the nonfinancial rewards of this arrangement, which are largely why we have continued to be landlords long after we needed to. Through careful interviewing of applicants, we have been most fortunate to find tenants who share our love of our special home and its solitude. While I'm sure that it is possible to have the tenants from hell that we first imagined as the norm, our experience has been just the opposite. And since our home is rather secluded, having an extra set of eyes and ears on the property has been a plus from a security point of view.

Now, as we grow ever nearer to retirement, it's comforting to know that our retirement income can be augmented by this rental income, an amount that neatly covers our monthly groceries and other incidentals. And unlike most other retirement income streams, this one is inherently hedged against inflation, since what we charge for rent steadily increases, as does the cost of bread and milk. On the other hand, should we require on-site health care or other living assistance as we grow older or should an aging family member need a close-by place to live, our guest apartment could always be converted for those purposes as well.

I recognize that not every house has the potential to generate rental income like ours, and renting out a room in your house, while an option worth considering, might cramp your style more than our rental unit does, with its separate entrance and private yard. But more home buyers should specifically search out houses that offer the potential for this or other types of income generation (e.g., in-home office or retail space), including proper-

ties that might otherwise seem out of your price range or that require some remodeling in order to create a hassle-free rental unit
(or two).

Homes that earn a living: a beautiful thing indeed. Now if I can
just get rid of the poltergeist living in the furnace.

6

Slow Down. You'll Get There Faster

*Everything in life is somewhere else, and you get there in
a car.*
—E. B. White

*We've been so busy keepin' up with the Jones
Four car garage and we're still building on
Maybe it's time we got back to the basics of love.*
—"Luckenbach, Texas (Back to the Basics of Love)," country-
western song by Chips Moman and Bobby Emmons

*Forget about a tree falling in the forest when no one's
there to hear it. What I really want to know is: Would
anyone drive a sixty-thousand-dollar automobile if no one
were there to see them in it?* —the Ultimate Cheapskate

"Jesus K. Riest! So what in the hell inspires somebody to ride
his goddamn bicycle all the way from Washington, D.C., to
New York City? I bin drunk before, but never that drunk."

The blurry-eyed quasi badass sitting across the double bar
from me had that harmless, one-too-many-but-docile-enough
quality, despite his outward bravado. Let the games begin.

"What? Oh, I needed to go to New York for some meetings.
Thought I'd take the fastest way," I responded, tipping back my
pint of Yuengling lager.

"Buddy, you're either full of shit or full of . . ." Alas, one of the great philosophical revelations of our times, lost for the ages because of an emergency visit to "the pisser."

Fortunately a friendlier-looking, more sober colleague took over for my urinator pal.

"Seriously, what do you mean, 'fastest way'? On a bicycle?" he said. "Are you jackin' with us or what? How fast can you pedal that thing?"

I went on to explain something Henry David Thoreau explained to me many years earlier in his monumental work *Walden*. In Henry's case it was the dollar equation of taking a train versus walking. Today I was expounding on the economics of a bicycle versus an automobile, but the logic was the same, another example of math confusion.

I explained that a bicycle is arguably the fastest machine ever invented. When you factor in the time it takes to earn enough money to buy a car (plus gas, insurance, etc.) or to buy a bicycle and get on down the road, the bicycle wins hands down.

(Although I decided not to make the story problem any more challenging than it already was for my bar mates—after all, it was happy hour—this very issue was examined in detail by the underappreciated social philosopher Ivan Illich, who had his heyday in the 1970s, when I was a sponge for this stuff. Not only does the bicycle come out on top in Illich's caloric / economic calculations, but by his similar reckonings the automobile averages less than five miles an hour when you factor in all the costs and the time spent earning the money to pay for it. You can read Illich's fascinating essay on the subject, "Energy and Equity," at http://reactor-core.org/energy-and-equity.html.)

Maybe it was the Jack Daniels he was drinking, but I felt a moment of profound awakening in my barfly brother.

"Huh," he said rather exhaustively, "I never thought of it that ways. Damn if it don't make sense, sorta."

A sixtyish-looking woman sitting two stools down took the Camel out of her mouth and uttered in an exhale, "Sh-e-e-e-t! Carl, you couldn't pump your skinny old ass up the next hill, let alone all the way to New York City."

The other patrons propped up along the bar erupted in laughter, making the requisite off-color remarks and predictable hip-thrusting gyrations in response to the words "pump," "Carl," and "skinny ass" being used in the same sentence.

A little annoyed by the laughs at his expense and, I thought, a little disappointed that our conversation was over, Carl put his empty glass on the bar. "Well, thanks for giving me something new to think about anyways. Let me buy you a beer, friend."

I accepted both the free beer and the new friend, thinking that I'd have had neither if I'd been traveling otherwise.

Nation on the Move

Of course Carl isn't alone. Most Americans suffer from what I call anal glaucoma when it comes to forms of transportation other than the automobile. That is, we just can't see ourselves dragging our asses down the road unless we're driving a car.

In 2000 we Americans owned 215 million cars, not quite 1 for every man, woman, and child, but of course kids don't drive a lot. That's twice as many per capita as in the 1950s, and the frequency of car ownership is expected to continue to grow, estimated to be 262 million vehicles by 2010. Our passion for our cars is one of the major reasons why since 1940 Americans alone have used up as much of the earth's mineral resources as all previous generations combined.

The automotive industry is a big, big business indeed. Nearly twenty billion dollars annually, just in advertising spending. The U.S. automotive industry as a whole is pushing the half-a-_trillion_-dollar mark in annual sales, so I guess that advertising is paying off. An estimated 20 percent of all advertisements in the United States are for cars or car-related products / services, and three of the six largest U.S. advertisers are automakers. With that kind of visibility, you don't even need to hide pictures of naked women in your ads.

We spend more on our cars (buying, driving, and maintaining them) than we spend on anything other than housing, nearly one-fifth of our income, or about 18 cents of every dollar we earn. The AAA says the average cost of owning a car in the United States is about $8,410 annually. That seems like a lot, but maybe not.

When you consider that we spend, on average, the equivalent of one-fifth of our typical work year (about 450 hours) sitting behind the wheel, maybe it's about right. And since most of that drive time is logged driving to and from work or in connection with our work, I guess there's a certain economic equilibrium to the math. That is, we spend as much time driving to / from work as we spend at work, earning the money we need in order to afford the car that we need, in order to get to work.

Economic equilibrium? Sounds more like a Money Step to me.

In fact it was the first Money Step I ever stumbled across when I was growing up, although I didn't know the proper name for it at the time. As my childhood chums turned sixteen and could get their driver's licenses, they inevitably did so and got jobs, so that they could buy cars, which they needed in order to get to work. If they were lucky, they could earn just enough money flipping burgers to make their car payments and pay for insurance and gasoline (although oftentimes _only_ enough gas to get to and from work).

Even when I was sixteen, when most of my gray matter was

consumed with the conundrum of which of Charlie's Angels I would most prefer to bed down with if given the chance, the lunacy of this proposition wasn't lost on me. Clearly at that early point in your working lifetime, you could just as well skip the job if you skipped the car. Of course, as your earning power increases, the balance starts to shift to where you are earning more (about 82 percent more, per the above) than it's costing you to drive to and from your job.

Nonetheless, there's a big old Money Step in there no matter how you slice it, one well worth looking into a bit further.

Live Without a Car?

That's the shocking proposition—heresy, really—we're challenged to consider in Chris Balish's refreshing and highly informative book *How to Live Well Without Owning a Car*. And I don't say "heresy" entirely in jest. After all, Balish dares question a basic tenet of American culture, the need to own your own four wheels.

While Balish recognizes that living car-free may not be practical for everyone (e.g., families with kids, those living in rural areas), he presents a compelling case for the rest of us on the basis of his own experience living car-free since 2003 and testimonials from more than a hundred others who have shed their wheels. Public transportation is of course a mainstay alternative, as it should be when you consider that 49 percent of us live in close proximity to a transit stop (2000 U.S. Census).

Balish also looks at other alternatives to car ownership, everything from walking, biking, and riding motorscooters to carpooling and car sharing. To evaluate if you're a likely candidate to go car-free, he suggests you ask yourself these six questions:

1. Can you get over your own ego (i.e., Will people think I'm a loser if I don't own a car?)?
2. Can you get to work reliably without a car?
3. Do you live in an urban area or a mixed-use development (either of which makes a car-free life more practical)?
4. Do you have access to public transportation?
5. Do you live in close proximity to amenities?
6. Are you flexible?

Even if going entirely car-free isn't an option for you, Balish offers strategies for curbing your use to the point where a two-car family (or more-car family) can cut back on the number of vehicles it owns. His suggestion of going car-free for a week—a sort of test driving of not driving—would be a perfect handicap to incorporate into your next fiscal fast. In fact buy yourself a doughnut (day-old, of course) if you do it!

Driving Ourselves . . . Insane?

Fun, fascinating, frightening facts about the environmental impact of our automobile addiction:

- **Remember the tragedy of the *Exxon Valdez* oil spill in Alaska?** Who doesn't? Thank God something like that hasn't happened again. Sorry for the bad news, but according to the National Academy of Sciences' Web site, it has. On average there are twenty-seven oil spills every day somewhere in the waters of the world. The *Valdez* spill doesn't even make the list of the top thirty largest.

- **And while we're speaking of the *Exxon Valdez*, . . .** every year in the United States we improperly dispose of sixteen times the amount of oil spilled by the *Valdez* (180 million gallons) by pouring it down drains and into the ground. Between that direct dumping and cars leaking oil in parking lots and roadways, experts say that the oil leaching out of each major U.S. city is roughly equivalent to a large tanker spill.

- **I love that Joni Mitchell song "Big Yellow Taxi." You know, the one with the lyrics "They paved paradise and put up a parking lot."** Well, it's not far from the truth, particularly if you think of Delaware as paradise. Every year in the United States we cover 1.3 million acres in blacktop, a space roughly equivalent to the size of the state of Delaware.

- **I hate it when people leave the refrigerator door hanging open while they're doing other things around the kitchen. But leaving it open for *six years*!** According to www.ChangingTheClimate.com, that's how much additional energy you're wasting every year when you drive a thirteen-miles-per-gallon SUV instead of an average new car. BTW, that's also equivalent to leaving a bathroom light burning for thirty years or a color TV turned on for twenty-eight years, in case you were wondering.

- **I was a typical kid, despite the way I turned out.** Or at least typical in terms of how I got to and from school. According to an article on the Web site Salon.com, 90 percent of kids who lived within a mile of school in the

1960s walked or bicycled to school. Today only 31 percent do. I was among that 90 percent. And when in my teenage years we moved to the country, five miles from my school, I still bicycled or took the bus. Other than a handful of emergencies when my parents needed to pick me up from school—like the time I accidentally vomited on Coach Sacstretcher from the top of the climbing rope in gym class—I was *never* driven to school by my parents. Today, though, the same *Salon* article says that about 30 percent of morning traffic congestion is caused by parents taking their kids to school. (But I guess it's understandable why kids can't walk or bike to school anymore, because in the 1960s there was no childhood obesity epidemic. Then again, kids walked or biked to school back then, which might explain why there was no childhood obesity epidemic . . .)

- **A fifty-thousand-mile-long train?** I'd hate to be stuck at a railroad crossing waiting for that one to pass. But the organization Environmental Defense says you'd need to burn all the coal that train could carry in order to generate the CO_2 emissions generated by U.S. cars and trucks in a year. That would be 314 million metric tons of CO_2, and the train would be long enough to circle the world, twice.
- **You may have heard of carbon dioxide** (CO_2). That's the stuff that Al Gore and others claim is causing global warming. I wouldn't be too worried about that doomsday stuff, though. Think on the bright side. Who knows? Maybe you'll be among the thirty thousand Americans who already die every year as a result of car emissions, and you won't even be around to deal with it.

How Much Are Your Wheels Really Costing You?

Even if you're not prepared to go car-free during your next fiscal fast, at least use it as an opportunity to dig into the true cost of owning and operating your automobile(s). I bet you'll have déjà vu sticker shock when you see the results.

Balish writes: "[T]he amount of money it costs to *buy* a car is very different from the amount it costs to *own* a car. . . . It's usually about double the purchase price." Yeah, that's right. By the time you compute the total costs involved in buying and operating a car (the so-called true cost to own, or TCO), it's usually about twice as much as the purchase price alone.

That means your fifty-five-thousand-dollar Cadillac Escalade escalades to more than a hundred thousand dollars. Your twenty-four-thousand-dollar Toyota Tundra is costing you a tundra more than you think at close to fifty thousand dollars. And a more "acura" picture of the true cost to own your thirty-eight-thousand-dollar Acura is closer to eighty thousand dollars.

To get an estimate of the TCO for your car—or your future car (if there's going to be a future car)—use the free TCO calculator at www.edmunds.com. You'll receive a customized analysis based on the make, model, year, and cost of your vehicle, new or used. The TCO calculator projects depreciation, financing, insurance, taxes / fees, fuel, maintenance and repair costs over a five-year period, on the basis of the assumption that you drive the vehicle fifteen thousand miles per year.

The edmunds.com calculator is a great resource, but even it doesn't take into account all the costs associated with keeping your four wheels on the road. For an even more accurate accounting, Balish provides an incredibly detailed worksheet in his book that includes everything from parking fees and tolls to the cost of speeding tickets and DWI arrests.

Four Keys to Curbing Car Costs

After—and *only* after—you've calculated the true cost to own your vehicle(s) and seriously considered ways to reduce your usage or even go car-free, here are some ways at least to minimize the dollars you're dropping along the highway as you drive on.

- **Drive 'em 'till they drop:** I was raised in a family that drove its cars until there was nothing left to drive. And I'm so glad I was. That simple lesson—an attitude really—has undoubtedly saved me more than if my parents had been in a position to set me up with a nice little trust fund at birth. In fact in our family we swore that we could still detect the new car smell after five years of ownership, and that was replaced by generations of equally satisfying smells, like Bandit, the cat that loved to ride in the car but always got sick, and beloved Grandpa Tex, who always smoked in the car even when Mom told him not to. I was reminded of the economic power of driving your car until it drops when I was playing around with the TCO calculator of edmunds.com. The calculator is misleading only in that it doesn't allow you to project TCO out beyond five years. If you were able to do that, you'd see the tremendous economic advantages of driving the same car for as long as it's roadworthy. Of course maintenance and repair costs are likely to increase as your car ages, but beyond five years your car will likely be fully paid off, so you'll no longer have car payments and financing charges, and you can probably save on insurance premiums by decreasing your collision and theft coverages, since your car is worth less. And the good news is that today's cars with the highest reliability ratings (see www.ConsumerReports.org), if properly maintained, can easily remain roadworthy for 150,000 miles or more; that's ten years or more, on the basis of edmunds.com 15,000 miles per year estimate. If the most expensive miles you ever drive are the first miles off the lot, when a new car's value plummets with instantaneous depreciation (see p. 151), then the least expensive miles you ever drive are those after your car is fully paid off and is still in good working order.

- **Recite these maintenance mantras:** I repeat my earlier mantra: Take care of your stuff, and your stuff will take care of you. When it comes to automotive maintenance, you need to recite that mantra as if you were a Hare Krishna disciple in an airport. A car is rather like the human body, with a multitude of interdependent parts; a little neglect can lead to a little problem, and a little problem can lead to major ones. Follow another mantra—well, more a commandment, really—Honor thy owner's manual, and learn to do the routine maintenance yourself. Not mechanical? Start with the nonmechanical: Keep your vehicle clean, inside and out; if you ever go to sell your car, a pristine appearance can be worth more than a purring engine. Move on to the basics: tire pressure, wiper blades, oil changes. (BTW, according to *Consumer Reports*, in most cases you need to change your oil only every seventy-five hundred

miles, not every three thousand as oil change merchants
would have you believe. Gee, maybe Grandpa Yeager
was on to something after all about vendors'
exaggerating the need for their own products / services?)
Graduate to the more advanced car care stuff if you're
so inclined; otherwise find a trustworthy mechanic to
keep your major maintenance work up-to-date.

- **Buy used but not abused:** Drive a new car off the sales
  lot and that instantaneous loss of value—a "new" car
  morphing into a "used" one—can easily drop the value
  by 20 percent or more, according to edmunds.com. So
  why not let some other guy take that hit and find
  yourself a used car in good condition? That's both the
  opportunity and the challenge. If we can assume that
  you're able to leave your vanity parked at home and
  don't insist on buying a new car, the question becomes
  how to avoid getting ripped off if you go with a used car.
  That's a legitimate concern, but one you can greatly
  reduce with some minimal effort. On the one hand, you
  know with 100 percent certainty that if you buy a new
  car you're going to experience a significant
  instantaneous decrease in value, and that should give
  you some chutzpah when shopping for a used car. On
  the other hand, the resources available to help educate
  used car shoppers are vastly superior to what they were
  pre-Internet. Three of the best sites for ranking
  dependability and customer satisfaction for used car
  models are www.jdpower.com, www.ConsumerReports.
  org, and www.edmunds.com. Once you've zeroed in on
  the model you're looking for, step two is to find it. In
  addition to examining local classified ads, check out
  these nationwide listings: www.usedcars.com,
  www.Car.com, www.CarsDirect.com. Before you close

the deal, it's definitely worth paying your own independent mechanic to check it out for you (expect to pay about fifty dollars). Also, consider investing twenty-five dollars in a vehicle history report from CARFAX.com that checks a specific vehicle's history (based on its vehicle identification number) to see if the car you're eyeing has ever been rebuilt, in a flood, or stolen. You can also buy some additional protection and peace of mind by doing business with a dealer (e.g., CarMax) that provides a certified inspection of all its used cars, warranties, and optional extended service plans, but those reassurances can really increase the price and, in my opinion, shouldn't eliminate the need to have your own mechanic take a look.

- **Think four wheels, hold the vanity:** I have a friend who once worked in the marketing department of an automobile manufacturer. He told me a story that initially struck me as unbelievable but that I've since learned is very common in that and other industries. Seems that his company launched a new vehicle that was greeted with lackluster sales, despite the fact that it got extremely good ratings for reliability, safety, and customer satisfaction and was very competitively priced at around nineteen thousand dollars. After conducting some focus groups and other market research, the company discovered that the new car was perfect, just what loads of consumers wanted. The problem was the price. The consumers who wanted the car were expecting to pay more for their vehicles, closer to thirty thousand dollars, so they weren't even considering my friend's new model. When the company increased the price of the car by ten thousand dollars (all profit to the company, of course), sales shot through the roof. The exact same car that had fizzled at nineteen thousand dollars was now priced at a level where people would buy it. The targeted customers wanted a more impressive car, or, more accurately, a car with a more impressive price tag. Think about that the next time you go car shopping (new or used), and leave your vanity parked at home.

Telecommuting: Make the Impossible Dream Possible

How many mph do you average during your daily commute? I'm talking about miles per hassle, not miles per hour. Or maybe that should be hassles per mile, if your commute is anything like the one mine used to be.

Here in the Washington, D.C., area, which consistently ranks among the worst commuting cities in the country, I became convinced by my daily personal observations that our problem is *not* insufficient highways or too many cars. Rather, I came to believe that the whole congestion problem at least in the D.C. area is actually due to just a handful of really lousy drivers.

Not only was there a car broken down and backing up traffic on the Woodrow Wilson Bridge every morning, but I began to notice that it looked like the same guy stalled out there every day. And the daily rear-ender on K Street was, I swear, the same lady in a blue minivan every day. Rather than build more roads, I theorized, we should just identify these dozen or so horrendous drivers and pay them to stay home, sort of like subsidized farming (i.e., paying farmers *not* to grow crops) but for spectacularly poor drivers. But I digress.

The truth is that traffic hassles on our daily commutes rank as one of our greatest complaints in life, at least for those of us living in urban areas. Since 1982 the U.S. population has grown 20 percent, but the time spent by commuters in traffic has grown 236 percent. (Maybe there's something to my handful of lousy drivers theory after all.)

Simple solution: Save some major scratch, and take a quantum leap forward in quality of life by working part-time or even full-time from home. I know, I know, the boss won't let you telecommute.

Bosses are like that. They want to make sure they're getting their money's worth. After all, they *know* you're working when they can see you sitting at your desk . . . consumed in a bidding war on eBay for that *My Mother the Car* lunch box you need to complete your personal collection.

That's the other thing I know about bosses: They want to make sure they're getting their money's worth.

Now that you know the true cost—in both dollars and quality of life—of your daily commute, you need to get aggressive if you're serious about convincing a reluctant boss to let you try telecommuting. Make him an offer he can't refuse. Next time you're due for a bonus or cost of living increase, what about telling the boss you want to skip the Money Step? That he can keep his extra alfalfa if you can work from home a couple of days each week?

As a former boss and a veteran of more employee salary reviews than I care to remember, I can tell you that that kind of proposition would definitely get my attention. Not just because of the possible salary savings but because of what it says about the employee. Here's someone with a strong set of priorities. Here's someone with a different way of thinking. Here's someone who has presented me with both the problem and the solution. Here's someone I want to make sure stays with my organization.

You know the size of the Money Step, how much it's costing you to commute to work every day in order to earn the money that you need in order to commute to work every day. The math (commuting cost versus potential salary increase) should be easy. And don't forget the endgame: Once you've proved to the boss that telecommuting really works, *then* you can hit her up for that raise you so boldly declined earlier—or maybe for more days working from home.

7

An Amish Guy's Guide to the Digital Age

*Oh, it was too much trouble, and besides, we needed a
clock in this room.* —Charity Daniels, my mother-in-law,
a kindred spirit when it comes to technology, explaining why
she's never hooked up the VCR the kids gave her for Christmas
three years ago, deciding instead to just use it for its clock in the
kitchen.

*I'm such a Neanderthal when it comes to technology. Like
the time a buddy of mine mentioned that he was going
out that afternoon to get a plasma screen. I felt awful for
him. "What is it?" I said. "Do you think you have
hepatitis?"* —the Ultimate Cheapskate

I am, as I openly admit throughout this book, a low-tech guy. I
don't know why that is. Maybe part of it is due to my inner
miser, whispering about another area of life where I can save
some money. But I also clearly lack whatever gene it is that en-
ables people to understand all that electronic-cyber-digital
stuff; that stuff that you can't see, smell, taste, or feel, that stuff
I can't even figure out where it is.

As Ralph H., one of my trusty Miser Advisers and a former
coworker, once said, "Yeager, you're the kind of guy we're trying to keep *off* the information superhighway! You're chugging

along at forty miles an hour in the left-hand lane, turn signal on the whole time!" This well-deserved berating was prompted by a most unfortunate incident that involved my spilling a cup of eggnog into my computer keyboard during the office Christmas party. It never worked quite the same after that.

I heard a certified "futurist" speak at a national convention a few years ago. (The fact that there is such a thing as a futurist, let alone one that is certified as such, impressed me immensely.) He spoke about the biggest challenges facing the world in the years ahead. After dismissing things like the looming energy crisis and global warming as mere flashes in tomorrow's pan, he informed the spellbound audience in a tone of absolute certainty that the single greatest challenge facing humankind in the years to come will be none other than bandwidth and, I gathered, some inherent limitations in that substance.

I was astounded and sat speechless in my chair until the auditorium was empty. The biggest threat to the continuation of humankind as we know it—the giant kahuna on the horizon of doom—and I had absolutely no idea what the speaker was talking about. *Bandwidth?*

Surprisingly, despite my low digital IQ, during the tech stock boom of the 1990s I developed a foolproof, albeit short-lived, method for picking tech stock winners. I don't own a lot of individual stocks, but a broker friend of mine would occasionally call me with a tip or two. The method I developed was simple: I would ask the broker to explain to me the business the company was engaged in prior to making my investment decision.

What I quickly discovered during that crazy economic time was that if I could understand even the slightest element of what the broker told me about the nature of the company's business, then I should definitely *not* invest. During those times it was the companies engaged in the development of cyber products and technological whatevers, the stuff that I couldn't understand even the first thing about, that were destined to chart new highs on the NASDAQ. Those were the stocks I bought, and with terrific results, at least for a while.

And then of course there's the cell phone, the high-tech hallmark of our generation. If I ever write another book, it will undoubtedly be about the cell phone phenomenon, primarily because I already have enough written material on the topic for at least a small volume. Of course I don't understand how cell phone technology works, nor do I own one. In fact one of my life goals is to live my remaining days without ever having to own one.

I realize that with the demise of telephone poles and cables this may simply be impossible at some point, and I also admit that cell phone technology and rates are becoming increasingly economical. No, my stance on cell phones is more about quality of life than about economics. You see, I've never really liked talking on the phone, so why would I want to inject more of it into my life? By contrast, I love woodworking, so if someone ever develops a cellular table saw, a wireless pocket-size one I can carry on my person at all times, count me in.

I remember the first time I came in contact with the then new technology of hands-free cell phones. I was traveling on business, and I saw a man dressed in business attire standing by himself in an airport lobby.

"Fuck! No! Fuck!" he shouted. "Christ! Shit! No!" he said, and then stomped his heels and strode off down the concourse.

As I continued my travels that week, I witnessed similar scenes in airport after airport along my route. As soon as I got home, I went rushing to see our family doctor, concerned that I too might fall victim to the outbreak of Tourette's syndrome that was obviously sweeping the nation's population of business travelers. First Legionnaires' disease, then SARS, now Tourette's: TRAVELERS BEWARE!

Oddly enough, I'm quite mechanically minded, despite my ineptitude in the field of technology. You often hear about people who have the misfortune of losing an eye or one of their limbs, and the intact counterpart becomes more capable to compensate for the disability. Such is the case with my mechanical ability and my technological disability.

For years I couldn't master the series of mouse maneuvers and keyboard strokes required to delete whole documents from my computer. What I discovered, though, was that my coffee mug was precisely the right height and my Swingline stapler exactly the right weight so that I could lean the stapler against the coffee mug, with the other end depressing the delete key. I could then enjoy a leisurely lunch, and when I returned, the unwanted documents would have entirely vanished.

If you need further proof of one faculty (the mechanical) compensating for the inferior performance of another (the technological), I offer this example from my Mother of Invention file. At one point during my career the organization I worked for decided that my efficiency would be exponentially improved if I worked entirely from a laptop computer. Apparently the company thought I would wake in the middle of the night, realize that I was using the laptop as a pillow, and bang out a little business correspondence before falling back asleep.

Well, the only problem with the laptop was that I could never, despite repeated tutorials, figure out how to hook it up to the printer and produce a hard copy. Invariably, sheepishly, I would have to bother one of the administrative assistants with a request: "Help me print?" Eventually I realized that my humiliation over this ritual harked back to my earliest memories of toilet training.

At any rate I was working late one night, needing to get a

document out via FedEx before nine. The masterpiece was finally complete, but I was the only one left in the office. How could I print out a hard copy? "Mommy, help me print!" Silence.

And then the mechanical faculty responded. Realizing that I was fairly competent with the Xerox machine and that the cord on my laptop was just long enough, I was able to photocopy the entire laptop screen as well as the top two rows of the keyboard, page after page. Shoving the copies in the FedEx envelope, I felt a strange, conflicted sense of victory, a combination of emotions. I had met a technological challenge, albeit with a method all too similar to photocopying your butt when you find yourself all alone some night in the office.

Go Figure

It's just an awful feeling that your privacy has been invaded. That something personal about you is just out there.
—General Wesley Clark, complaining about cell phone records being available for sale online (ABC Evening News, February 6, 2006)

America's two hundred million plus cell phone users—or Cellulites, as I call them—are up in arms over their calling records being made available online to anyone willing to pay for them. Imagine that, people who insist on sharing their private conversations with everyone within earshot concerned about privacy.

Of course Cellulites also applauded recent federal legislation mandating a national do not call list. This, just as the U.S. cell phone industry topped one hundred billion dollars annually. Having involuntarily eavesdropped on thousands of cell phone calls over the years, I believe that most Cellulites crave phone conversation of any kind, regardless of whom they're calling or who's calling them. I would think they'd be lobbying Congress for a mandatory must call list.

In fact I've been conducting an informal survey of my own, and I've found that about 90 percent of the time the first word spoken by one party to every cell phone call made is the same word: "nothin'." Caller / recipient: "What's going on?" Response: "Nothin'." Caller / recipient: "What are you doing [besides calling me or being called by me]?" Response: "Nothin'." Thank God we have the technology to communicate vital information at will; now, if we just had something to say.

How can so many Americans love talking on the phone when at the same time phone-based jobs (e.g., telemarketers, receptionists, telephone operators) consistently rank among the least desirable jobs in our society? Go figure.

Butt Technology Spending Is No Laughing Matter

My own technological impotence aside, tech-savvy Americans are snatching up electronic gadgets, computer paraphernalia, and telecommunications technology at a mind-numbing rate. Personal U.S. spending on these goods and services totaled more than $260 billion in 2004, significantly more than the gross domestic products of all the countries in Central America combined. As a nation we now spend more than twice as much each year on these playthings as we do on higher education. After all, who needs a college education when you have TiVo?

Carol W. is a self-proclaimed Born Again Cheapskate. As one of my Miser Advisers and a successful freelance graphic artist, she tells a sad but familiar story of tech addiction.

"I told myself that I needed it for my business, but I knew deep inside I really just wanted it for myself," she says, lovingly stroking her HP Special Edition Notebook with Intel Centrino mobile technology, Bluetooth wireless connectivity, and 12-Cell lithium ion battery.

"At first it was small stuff. Like a cordless mouse or some extra RAM. You know, things I could afford to pay for out of the business's cash flow or what I was taking out for myself." She sighs. I feel sorry for having asked her to tell me the story, but she insists that it will be good for her recovery.

"Then I'd have a slump in my business, but the new technology just kept coming. Every time I heard about a new product I'd convince myself that I needed it in order to stay competitive. It wasn't a question of whether or not I'd buy it; it was just a question of when. Eventually, when I couldn't afford to pay cash, I got out the old credit card, and that was the beginning of the end." She pushes her HP Notebook away, like a recovering alcoholic pushing away a shot of Jack just before it gets the best of him.

Thankfully, Carol W. now has her financial house in order, rivaling even the Ultimate Cheapskate when it comes to limiting tech spending. "The only gadget I've bought in the last six months is a portable CD player," she says proudly, "and I got that at a yard sale for two bucks. The problem is it skips so badly that I can only listen to Bob Dylan on it, since it really doesn't make any difference."

Borrowing a Parchment from the Amish

Carol W.'s inspiring story of kicking her tech-spending addiction got me thinking. We truly have become a culture addicted to the latest technology. As Carol said, for most of us it's not a question of whether or not we'll buy the tech gadget du jour; it's just a question of when.

That mentality is obviously helping drain our bank accounts, but I started thinking about the broader impact it has on our lifestyles, even beyond the money. I began thinking about the Amish, who I'd always heard spurned technology in pursuit of a simpler life, and I wondered if they might have some lessons to teach the rest of us. (Plus, I admit to follicle envy; I've always admired guys who can effortlessly grow robust quantities of facial hair.)

It's a little difficult to find out just what the Amish believe and why. There's not a great deal published about their lifestyle and beliefs. In attempting to research the Amish a bit more for this book, I found myself wishing there were a monthly magazine, maybe titled something like *Amish Life* or *Ye Horse and Buggy,* a quick read I could pick up at the newsstand for an overview and updates on that community's current affairs.

I digressed even further in my thinking for a moment, imagining that such a publication, if it existed, would include the obligatory section of personal ads. I began thinking about how those ads would read: "Me: AGATT (All Gingham All the Time). Love candlelight dinners and candlelight in general. You: BNZ (Buttons, No Zippers). Willing to grow a beard. Must like horses and / or long walks."

Alas, apparently no such publications exist, so the quest for answers to my questions about the Amish required a short road trip. Fortunately, and somewhat surprisingly, there's a fairly large Amish population in southern Maryland, not far from where I live just outside the urban sprawl of Washington, D.C. As I pointed my Toyota pickup truck southbound one chilly January morning, I had a bit of trepidation about the outing. I didn't have any interviews lined up in advance. After all, I couldn't very well phone ahead, given that the Amish don't own phones.

I had my intended interview questions dutifully written down in my spiral notepad on the seat next to me, but as I drove south, I struggled with how I would phrase my initial inquiry, the one to gas station attendants and other locals along the way as I sought out some Amish folks I could interview. Every possible line I rehearsed in my mind seemed awkward, even sexually suggestive. What would I ask? "Hey, buddy, know where I can find me some Amish?"

My anxiety was short-lived, as I'd no sooner crossed the line into St. Mary's County when I spotted a conclave of horse buggies parked in a special horse-'n'-buggy parking area in front of the Hook-n-Hanger Thrift Store.

St. Mary's is Maryland's southernmost county, on the tip of a peninsula that ends where the Potomac River joins the Chesapeake Bay. During the Civil War, despite the fact that Maryland remained part of the Union, this part of the state was a hotbed of southern sympathizers. That came in handy when John Wilkes Booth fled through these same farm fields and marshlands after shooting President Lincoln at Ford's Theater. Dr. Mudd's home and the Surratt Tavern, hideouts for Booth during his flight south, remain popular historic sites today.

It's also home of one of America's first settlements, St. Mary's City (first settled in 1634), and increasingly this region is home to folks with lifestyles and incomes incompatible with the upscale urbanization blowing south from the nation's capital. As D.C. area property prices soar and new subdivisions extend their tentacles out in every direction almost overnight, semi-rural southern Maryland has benefited from becoming home to an eclectic population of refugees fleeing farther and farther south of Washington, following Booth's escape route of 140 years ago. Today these counties are home to poorer and middle-income African Americans, first-generation immigrants from countries around the globe, the Amish, and even some of us cheapskates.

And did I mention rednecks? Parking my econo-size Toyota pickup next to a Ford F-250, a monster truck that could easily haul my miniature vehicle in its cargo bed, I glanced at its bumper sticker: "My Other Car Is a BIG DICK." Ah, subliminal messaging southern Maryland style.

Knew I Shouldn't Have Shaved This Morning

Although I'd actually thought about my wardrobe selection for the day (highly unusual for me), my Levi's and the earth-tone shirt and jacket I was wearing suddenly seemed gauche. I swiped the red ball cap off my head as I made my way across the parking lot toward the buggies. "Need to tone it down," I thought, "if I'm going to hang with the Amish."

Just as I was approaching the Hook-n-Hanger, a group of five bearded men were exiting the store. Concerned that they might be heading off, I quickened my pace, only to see through the plate glass windows that their wives remained inside the store, pawing enthusiastically through the mounds of secondhand merchandise.

"Good," I thought, "the menfolk are headed out to tend to the horses, a perfect bonding opportunity for me." Although I've never really spent any time around horses, or Amish men for that matter, I imagined that I could lend a hand feeding them some hay and wiping down their hindquarters. The horses, that is.

To my surprise, the Amish men pulled up short of the buggy

corral, and an older man in the group produced a pack of Marlboro 100's and passed them around. Wow, cultural epiphany.

By then I was upon them, hand thrust out, smile bursting from my face, a conditioned response to the years I spent in the fundraising trade.

"Hello! Er, are you Amish, by any chance?"

As soon as I said it, I realized the absurdity, verging on patronization, of what I'd just said. Five bearded guys, dressed in identical black hats, blue work shirts, and black pants supported by suspenders, were standing next to their horses and buggies. What did I expect them to say? "No. We're Chippendale dancers on our way to a bachelorette party."

Fortunately the older man in the group, the one with the smokes, immediately established himself as having far more grace, humility, and intelligence than I can ever hope to have.

"Vel', yess, sirr, we'r," offering me the pack of Marlboros, which I declined.

Jake's pleasant smile, tempered with a hint of mischief, and his sparkling eyes, immediately set me at ease. I babbled something about writing a book, always ♥'ing the Amish, etc. Eventually I formed a halfway coherent question about my interest in the Amish's stance on technology.

"No, ve try not to yewss it. No moore than ve 'ave to." Jake responded in a thick German accent, this, despite the fact I would learn that Jake and the others were at least third-generation Americans. It struck me that there could be no greater evidence of the Amish's success in sheltering their lifestyle and preserving their convictions than their ability to maintain this dialect in a rapidly urbanizing area of the eastern seaboard.

As we talked, the two younger Amish men climbed aboard one of the buggies and rolled out across the parking lot toward the busy highway. Oddly, like a mother fearful for her child trying out the training wheels on his new bike, I wanted to warn them about there being cars on that road.

Jake, Seth, Zeb, and I lingered for a few minutes, they waiting for their wives to emerge from the Hook-n-Hanger, I thinking about how I wished I had a cool first name like theirs. A tight-lipped trio, for sure, not unfriendly by any means, but not the kinds of guys you could chat it up with.

I did manage, though, to confirm my basic understanding about the Amish belief system, at least when it comes to technology. In an attempt to humble themselves before God, the Amish think long and hard about doing anything that might suggest hubris or complacency. This includes self-imposed limitations, but not total prohibitions, against the use of modern technology.

For example, the Amish will use telephones when necessary, but will not own one, sometimes even having a pay phone specially installed just across the road from their house. They have a network of non-Amish contacts who will shuttle them to / from destinations in a motorized vehicle for specific purposes (e.g., large shopping trips), but they will not own cars or trucks themselves.

The Amish are sometimes criticized for apparent inconsistencies like this, but the important thing I learned is that before allowing any specific technological advance into their community (or before deciding to exclude it), the Amish rigorously contemplate the effect a given piece of new technology will have on their lives. How simple. How refreshing. How different from the rest of us.

"Ya, da English [I found out later that almost anyone non-Amish, including me, is considered English] don' unnerstand 'r ways." So true, Jake.

Take a Bye, Don't Make a Buy

I came away from my afternoon with Jake and the boys inspired by the example the Amish set for the rest of us with their simple but satisfying lifestyle. While their belief system isn't predicated on saving money, but on humbling one's self before God, it clearly has the additional benefits of preserving a simple quality of life and lessening one's dependency on money.

I'd grown up in an area with a small Amish community, and I thought about the thirty-five years that had passed since then. Their lives had changed very little since the 1970s, or even the 1870s for that matter. My life, and the lives of everyone else I grew up with, had changed immensely in terms of what we own, the technology we rely on every day, and the impact all that has on our lifestyle.

While the scope of this change was immense on the surface, it clearly hasn't translated into a quantum leap forward for us when it comes to happiness or quality life, relative to the Amish. When I factor in the negatives, ranging from predators stalking our children on the Internet to movies now being interrupted by ringing cell phones, it's not clear to me whether there's been a net gain at all. Depending on how you weigh the factors, you might even conclude that the Amish have lapped us.

Nonetheless, as I drove home, I wasn't prepared to fully relinquish my "English" ways and become Amish, this, despite encouragement from Jake, in response to an attempt at humor on my part. I had joked as I was getting ready to leave that I couldn't convert because I didn't have enough capacity for facial hair. Squinting with one eye as he carefully studied my boyish complexion, he finally delivered his prognosis: "I'l come, i'l come."

Then, as I stroked the imaginary stubble on my chin, it hit

me: Maybe there had been some Amish in me all along. During my years of managing nonprofit organizations I coined the phrase "Take a bye, don't make a buy," which became my standard response when an enthusiastic staffer pushed me to spend our limited resources on the latest generation of new office technology. I realized there was something Amish-esque about that management philosophy, and I swore I could see a five o'clock shadow when I looked at myself in the rearview mirror, yet it was barely three-thirty in the afternoon.

Needing to remain effective and competitive, but working with limited financial resources, nonprofits can't simply do without new technology, à la the Amish. Nor can they afford to invest continually in each new generation of technology as it becomes available, the common approach in the for-profit sector and the modus operandi of most American consumers. Rather, savvy nonprofit managers continually evaluate the worth of new technology, using a thought matrix that takes into account not just the cost and possible applications of a new technology but other key factors like the projected obsolescence time frame, missed opportunity costs (by both investing or not investing), and, most important, the cost savings accrued by skipping a generation (or two)—that is, the bye factor.

Come, Let Us Reason Together

In the nonprofit organizations I've helped manage, I insisted that we apply this thought process to any potential technology purchases, regardless of whether the organization was relatively prosperous or poor at the time. Usually to the chagrin of some young staffer, who insisted that his job would simply be made impossible unless we immediately invested in the latest software upgrade or digital whatever, I would close the door to my office and work through the decision-making process with the anxious employee in tow.

First we would look at the direct cost of the proposed new piece of technology. Knowing my frugal management style, even newer employees usually came armed with neatly labeled files containing information on purchase cost. Then the Socratic dialogue began.

What about competing quotes? What about bundling the purchase with other scheduled buys from preferred vendors? What about buying it used or getting it donated, since we were a charitable organization and donors (or even "bargain sellers") could get tax write-offs? What about other costs: installation, service contracts, training, peripherals?

Admittedly these types of questions were routine on my part, whether we were buying paper clips or a new computer. "Just doing my job," I'd tell the flummoxed staffer sitting uneasily in the chair across the desk from me. But in the case of proposed technology purchases, the fun was only beginning.

After asking my young colleague to tell me, in language even I, the Amish Guy of Technology, could understand, why the purchase was necessary and provide examples of what it would allow him to do that he couldn't currently do, I invariably had some more questions: Have you ever used this technology before? How long has it been available? Does our competition already have this capacity, and if so, how has it used it to its advantage? What's the worst thing that will happen if we don't buy it? What's the best thing that will happen if we do? What's the cost of the same technology likely to be a year from now?

In the case of proposed technology purchases, the final two considerations—projected obsolescence and the related bye factor—were the most important, and usually the most difficult, to determine. When I asked about obsolescence—How long do we expect to be able to use this?—the staffer usually responded with a puzzled look. Common answers included "Well, it comes with a lifetime guarantee" and "This is state of the art, Jeff"—in other words, nonanswers, merely recitations of marketing claims.

Rarely did even the most capable staff member expand his research of the new product beyond the marketing information provided by the manufacturer. Now, I've yet to see a manufacturer make this type of claim in its promotional information: "The VX7000 is the most advanced state-of-the-art product of its kind. There's truly nothing like it on the market today, but we want to let you know that in five months our company will introduce the VX8000, which will be vastly superior to the VX7000 in every way."

But the undeniable fact is that this is exactly how the technology industry operates, because of both the rapid evolution of the technology itself and, dare I say it, the desire on the part of these companies to churn their market base as frequently as possible. Why come out with a new and improved product only once a year if you can release a (partially) new and (partially) improved version of the product three times a year? Those clients with the financial resources, and who succumb to your marketing efforts, will pony up three times instead of once.

So the concept of taking a bye, rather than always making a buy, depends on getting good, objective information about the projected obsolescence life span of a piece of technology and evaluating that information in the context of this question: What will happen if we skip this level and move directly to the next level(s) once it becomes available?

Occasionally we concluded that it would not be cost-effective to take a bye—for example, if a competing organization already had such technology and was likely to use it to lure away our members, supporters, or sponsors. In other cases, we found that if we did not invest in the next level (e.g., expansion of our phone system at a critical juncture), we would be unable to accommodate any future growth.

But in the vast majority of cases, following this type of cost-benefit analysis, we found that we were far ahead on the financial scoreboard by taking a bye rather than making a buy. That's not to say that we became Amish, forgoing all new technology. In fact on occasion we truly had state-of-the-art technology, but *only* on occasion, not continually.

The impact: a net savings of tens of thousands of dollars annually with little or no loss of productivity, efficiency, or competitiveness.

How to Get Supercharged Returns by *Not* Investing

The challenge—in business as well as personal life—is to develop the critical judgment, based on solid research, to decide when to take a bye. The trade and consumer media, not the marketing material provided by manufacturers, are where you should be researching new technology. And if your appetite for a new product is whetted by such promotional material, do yourself a favor and research that company's competitors. See what they think about the product you're salivating over. If they're not already marketing a product that they claim is superior, that's the company you want to talk to.

Ask it what it has coming down the pipeline. Chances are that it plans to launch something very shortly that will make you feel sorry if you buy from its competitor now. If you take a little time to do this research, you'll probably find yourself talking yourself out of buying now because you'll realize that a new, improved version is just around the corner.

While spending procrastination—putting off until tomorrow what you want to buy today—is a strategy endorsed throughout this book, in no area of consumer spending is this advice more important than when it comes to technology. That's because a tech product is likely to be useless long before it actually ceases to function. So while I counsel that you should drive your car as long as it continues to get you there, at some point a computer may continue to run but will be incompatible with the technology used by everyone else.

When you're investing in new technology, you have to take into account this likelihood of premature death because of planned obsolescence. On the surface, planned obsolescence doesn't sound like good news. But it results in a tremendous savings opportunity if you follow my advice for taking a bye. By opting out of certain next generations of technology, the savings you accrue are actually accelerated by the shortened life cycle of that technology. In other words, because technology is becoming obsolete at such a warp speed rate, the return on noninvestment is that much greater. Think of it as the difference between interest compounding daily and annually.

New, Improved, *and* Cheaper

Plus—and it's a big plus—the cost of a new piece of technology commonly *drops* after its initial introduction. Market demand increases competition, prices drop, and those who buy early tend to pay more than those who show some restraint when a product is first introduced.

This happens all the time in the electronics industry, as first-generation products from flat screen TVs to CD players cost more, even in fixed dollars, than subsequent versions of the same products. And often the later versions are significantly improved, with the bugs worked out from previous models and enhancements added. Talk about RONI! If you have to be the first kid on your block to own the new digital humdinger, you usually end up paying more and getting an inferior product than if you'd just had some willpower and waited a little while.

As I said earlier in this book, I had a reputation as the Titan of Tightwads in the nonprofit organizations I helped manage. But as I hope my coworkers will attest, I also had a reputation as a bighearted, fairly well-liked miser boss. Nonetheless, if I held court with a staffer who simply refused to acknowledge the inherent wisdom of the "take a bye, don't always make a buy" concept that I've just explained, I used to end the little chat in my office with the following: "Hey, before you go, a friend of mine has a bunch of Betamax tapes he's trying to sell. You interested?"

✎ The Betamax Quiz: Avoid Buying Yesterday's Technology Today and Regretting It Tomorrow

Although compared with most Americans, I spend very little on electronic gadgets and other new technology, the few items I do buy are among the most likely culprits to be in the lineup when it comes time for my annual "What the Hell Was I Thinking" Audit? (see Chapter 2). Between opiate-strength advertising and planned obsolescence, buyers' remorse is almost inevitable in the consumer electronics and technology marketplaces.

If you're really addicted to spending on electronics or other technology, try supplementing your annual spending audit with this special Betamax Quiz to thwart regrettable technology purchases before you make them. Answer these questions before you go shopping.

1. **How long have you wanted this item?**
   - *One week or less:* Guys, take the condom out of your wallet, and put it on your wallet. Women, padlock your purses. Never buy any discretionary technology without adhering to the mandatory thirty-day waiting period (see Chapter 3).
   - *One month or so:* Conduct your own focus group of one (see Chapter 4). Think about what you're really thinking about the next time you see an advertisement for this product. If it's sex, unless you're shopping for battery-powered love toys, put away your money.
   - *Six months or so:* Spend an hour researching the item / technology again, this time using sources *other* than information provided by the manufacturer. Any mention of a new, improved version coming soon?
   - *More than six months:* DANGER ZONE! This is the period when you *should* be most likely to make a purchase. And if you've followed the prescribed steps, it might in fact be the right move. As a final step, talk with someone who already owns one. Any buyers' remorse yet on his part?
   - *As long as I can remember:* And has your life been worse because of not owning it?

2. **Have you owned one of these before (e.g., an earlier version)?**
   - *If so:*
     - Were you satisfied with it? Why / why not, and how will this one be different / better?

- Any buyers' remorse the first time around?
- Is it still usable? If so, see Questions 3 and 4, below.
- *If not:*
  - Beware!
  - Carefully follow the steps outlined under Question 1.
  - Remember the Amish. Do you really want to head down this new road in the first place? Think about the impact this new technology will have on both your lifestyle and finances before you invite it in.

3. **What's the worst thing that will happen if you don't buy it? What's the best thing that will happen if you do?**

4. **Think about taking a bye. What will be the impact of skipping this generation of new technology and, at a later time, going directly to the next (new and improved!) level when it becomes available?**
   - Research the projected life span of the item and evaluate its cost, using the thought process outlined in this chapter.
   - Recognize the advantages, as well as any disadvantages, of taking a bye. For example, will it be more costly or impossible to upgrade in the future if you skip a step now?

FINALLY . . . ALWAYS REMEMBER *BETAMAX:*

B e aware of your compulsion to buy the latest technological gadgets.

E xamine your triggers for responding to tech advertising.

T hink about the last time you bought something that you regretted later.

A cknowledge that tech products are likely to become obsolete in a matter of months or even weeks and that prices often drop after a product is first introduced.

M ake a list of ten things you could do with the money instead.

A ct on your urges to buy only after completing the Betamax Quiz.

X erox a copy of your butt, and send it to me for a coffee table book I'm working on. [Now that's subliminal messaging!]

Power to the People

While the Amish choose to live without electricity, two billion people around the globe have no choice. That's right. About 30 percent of the world's population lives off the grid. Think about that the next time you're freaking out when there's no hair dryer in your hotel room.

Bringing power to the people is one of the biggest humanitarian challenges facing humankind today. The digital divide is widening the gap between rich and poor like nothing the world has experienced before.

Bringing electricity to these two billion folks via traditional energy sources (e.g., coal, oil, hydro) is an immense, costly, and environmentally risky proposition. Increasingly even old-school energy giants like British Petroleum (BP) are convinced that the solution for those living off the grid is going to be found in solar energy. BP recently contracted to bring solar power to approximately four hundred thousand households in rural areas of the Philippines.

How costly would it be to provide solar power to those two billion souls currently living without electricity? According to the World Bank's International Finance Corporation, a solar home system capable of powering a couple of lights and a small appliance or two currently costs about $550 and has a life expectancy of about twenty years. If such a system could provide basic electrical service to, say, a family of four, then half a billion units (i.e., two billion individuals = five hundred million families of four) would cost about $275 billion.

That's a lot of money, for sure. After all, it's almost half of what Americans spend eating in restaurants each year.

8

Now *That's* Entertainment

The view from the top of the mountain is the same, no matter how much money you have.

—the Ultimate Cheapskate

Give me golf clubs, fresh air and a beautiful partner, and you can keep the clubs and the fresh air. —Jack Benny

Many men go fishing all of their lives without knowing that it is not fish they are after. —Henry David Thoreau

What turns you on? No! I don't mean like that! (But if you care to send me those thoughts and / or photos privately by e-mail at CheapThrill4Me@aol.com, I can't stop you. Nor do I have an e-mail filter installed, in case you're wondering.)

What I mean is: What are your passions in life? What do you enjoy doing when you're not busy making and spending money? Provided that you have any time left over, that is.

If spending money, at least spending money on more stuff, is your answer, then you're likely to be pretty unhappy. Or so says Harvard Professor of Psychology Daniel Gilbert in his afore-applauded book *Stumbling on Happiness*.

Gilbert makes the case that things—stuff, objects, chattel—tend to lose value over time. Not necessarily monetary value (although I'd argue for that position in most cases), but in terms of the value to their owner / purchaser, the degree to which they continue to satisfy and, yes, provide a sense of happiness. That's only common sense given all the things we buy that we immediately regret and the many others that break, wear out, or become obsolete. Stuff: There's really no future in it.

On the other hand, experiences, as opposed to things, tend to retain their value—or in some cases even increase in value—over time. How many gifts (birthday, Christmas, Chanukah, you name it) can you recall from your childhood, and how many do you still use or enjoy today? But how many memories from those same family celebrations and holidays are still with you today? And how many of those memories are even more poignant than way back when?

So experiences tend to endure and sometimes even appreciate in value, while stuff tends to decrease in value over time. Of course experiences can cost a lot of jack too, just like stuff. Have you priced a Kenya safari lately?

But I've generally found that cost seems to have little to do with the value of experiences over time. For example, it cost nothing for my aunt Nadine's blouse to miraculously fly open at my thirteenth birthday party, as she coquettishly sliced me a piece of chocolate devil's food cake, yet I still remember it vividly (and frequently) to this day.

The Renaissance Miser

I opined earlier on the simple but oh-so-life-changing realization that if time is money, then money is time. Ergo, spend less money and you'll have more time. More time to do more, see more, be more. More time to have more experiences.

Following on the insights of Professor Gilbert, let me suggest that the breadth and diversity of the experiences we put ourselves through while we're here on earth are equally as important as the depth of those experiences and vastly more important than how much we spend on those experiences. In fact, when it comes to spending money on most types of experiences, like travel, learning different skills, becoming a better human being, once again, the more money you spend, the less you'll have to show for it.

That's why with the time of my own life, I'm striving to become a Renaissance Miser, a well-rounded, experience-schooled, caring human being who values time and the things you can do with it more than money and the things you can buy with it.

I don't for a minute profess to be able to tell you how to spend the time of your life, and that's not the intent of this chapter or this book. But I do want you to think about some ways you can maximize that time by minimizing some Money Steps and in the process broaden your life experience. Who knows? Maybe you'll become a Renaissance Miser yourself.

Pick Your Passions Prudently

Now that's a crazy statement. After all, passion means having a strong emotional attraction to something or someone, an attachment that traditionally defies reason. It's something we have no control over, something we cannot explain, something we can no more choose than we can deny.

Or can we?

There's not a lot of science on the issue, at least that I've been able to unearth with regard to my specific interest in the topic—namely, can you choose or kick-start the hobbies, activities, and other interests that become the predilections for your free time?

I believe you can, or at least you can sure as heck try. And if I'm right or even if I *might* be right, why not spend a few minutes thinking about those choices? After all, they might very well be the difference between your financial self-sufficiency and your financial ruin, inasmuch as each year Americans spend almost $350 billion on recreational activities.

Five Ways to Fall in Love

Maybe you can't dictate all your passions and interests in life—it would be a shame if you could—but here are some tips for helping shape and direct at least some of those pursuits:

- **Teach your children well:** There's no denying the fact that our parents' interests and other experiences we're exposed to early in life help shape our passions and tastes as adults. No, I'm not talking about my aunt Nadine's blouse again! (But, Aunt Na-Na, if you're reading this and want to send me anything, that's CheapThrill4Me@aol.com.) Can't afford to give your kids a fat trust fund to help them with the financial burdens of life? Sure you can. Encourage the kids in your life to pursue interests, like those I'll discuss in a minute, that are affordable and healthy and will save them money throughout their lives. By doing so, you'll be giving them a sort of nonmonetary investment portfolio, a stock portfolio of interests and skills that will save them big bucks as adults. If in the end they adopt some pricey pastimes as well, so be it, but some frugal interests will help them better afford the ones that aren't.

- **Take a ride on the Reading:** Whether you're eight or eighty, force yourself to pick up at your local library a book on one of the thrifty life hobbies listed on page 191. Why not? It's free. TIP: If you're just starting out and looking for inspiration, try books that are long on beautiful photographs and short on words. The current trend in what a friend of mine calls hobby porn— erotically gorgeous, full-color books about cooking, gardening, home improvement, arts and crafts, and even auto mechanics—is sure to pique your interest and leave you wanting to learn more.

- **What are friends for?:** Do you have a friend who's a great cook or has a green thumb (but preferably *not* a green-thumbed cook)? Ask him to cut you in on the action next time he's practicing his craft. Chances are he'll be flattered and you'll be inspired to learn from someone you already feel comfortable with and enjoy spending time around.

- **Got class?:** Whether it's a noncredit course at the local community college, an online tutorial, or a how-to show on public television or video, resolve to expose yourself at least once a month. No! I don't mean like that! (But remember, that's CheapThrill4Me@aol.com.) I mean, spend a few hours learning something new, a skill you'll enjoy and one that will save you money.

- **The apprentice:** You don't need an apprenticeship with Donald Trump to get motivated or learn something valuable. In addition to free on-the-job-training by volunteering with a nonprofit organization (see "When I Grow Up, I Want to Be a Volunteer!," page 184), what about offering your gruntwork services for a chance to hang out in the kitchen at your favorite restaurant or help during the holiday rush at your neighborhood florist shop? You'll learn lots, and I'll bet you'll even get a discount the next time you patronize the establishment.

When I Grow Up, I Want to Be a Volunteer!

When I grow up, I want to be a (fill in the blank)!

Do you remember the sense of exhilaration you once had when you filled in that blank? And then it happened. You grew up.

For most of us, "astronaut" became "accountant," "firefighter" became "financial analyst," and "veterinarian" became "veteran of more sales meetings, performance reviews, and downsizings than you thought humanly possible" (aka "a dog's life for a dog lover").

Oh, well, it's too late to do anything about it now. Or is it? As you reclaim the time of your life by curing your spending addiction, consider a new career opportunity: as a volunteer.

It's true that volunteering is its own reward, and we should do it primarily because others need our help, but it's also a chance to peek inside career fields that interest us, to roll up our sleeves and learn something new, all while doing good. OK, so maybe you can't be a volunteer astronaut, but I bet there's a science museum or planetarium near you that needs volunteers (www.museumsusa.org). Firefighter? Almost 75 percent of all U.S. firefighters, more than eight hundred thousand in all, are volunteers (www.nvfc.org). Animal lovers need look no further than their local Humane Society (www.hsus.org) or other animal rescue organization for their fix of puppy love; volunteers are the lifeblood of nearly all such groups.

Nearly sixty-five million Americans say they volunteer at least once each year. That seems like a lot, but when you consider that there are more than 1.5 million nonprofit organizations in the United States that need their help, our current volunteer workforce is stretched thin.

When I worked as a professional in the nonprofit sector, people sometimes asked whether I'd prefer them to make a financial contribution or volunteer their time. My answer was always the same: Yes. Nearly all nonprofit organizations need and deserve a gift of both your time and your treasure. And the sense of satisfaction you receive by giving both is exponentially increased.

Even though successful nonprofit organizations increasingly, and wisely, rely on professional staffs in order to deliver their missions, volunteers help keep those organizations grounded in those missions and augment both their workforces and capacities. Smart nonprofit organizations understand that and increasingly use volunteers in more specialized, creative, and challenging positions than in the past. It's also been my experience that volunteers, when they have a positive experience with an organization, become its greatest goodwill ambassadors and public spokespeople.

But just like with a paying job, not every volunteer experience is a positive one. It needs to be the right match, or else the volunteer, the organization, or both end up unhappy. Some things to consider before you sign on as a volunteer:

- **The interview:** Yes, that's right, *the interview.* Insist on sitting down with the person you'd be reporting to if you accept a volunteer position and having a conversation not unlike the one you'd have if you were applying for a paid position. If the organization or supervisor is reluctant to do so, beware; you can likely expect an inexact boss if you accept.
- **Time commitment / schedule:** Organizations have the right to expect volunteers to be prompt and conscientious about their work schedules, so don't expect that you can

show up whenever you feel like it. But volunteers have a right to have those time requirements spelled out in detail before they commit. Be very cautious if an organization is vague about when you'll be needed or how much time it expects of you.

- **Special skills / training:** This should be a win-win situation. Volunteering is a great (and free!) way to learn new skills, and many nonprofit organizations pride themselves on the training opportunities they afford their volunteers; be sure to ask about them in the interview. At the same time, be honest about the skills you do (and don't) have and those that you are (and aren't) prepared to bring to a volunteer position. For example, I have considerable experience as a professional fundraiser—something in high demand by most groups—but I'm no longer interested in working with organizations in that capacity. In short, don't mislead and don't be misled.

- **Work environment / culture:** In my experience, this is the most likely deal maker or deal breaker. Just follow your instincts. Do you like the people you met during the interview? Do they seem like the kind of people you'd enjoy spending time with socially, since volunteering is a blend of social and professional interactions? Does the work environment seem too professional or too casual for your tastes? Are you convinced that the organization and the people you'll be working with share your commitment to the mission of the organization?

- **Future prospects:** "So where do you see yourself in five years?" is a question commonly asked at job interviews but, unfortunately, rarely broached in talks with potential volunteers. Some volunteers eventually hope to find paid employment with the organization or in the field, or the other way around; some organizations intend to cultivate volunteers for more challenging or governance positions down the line. But sometimes a volunteer simply wants the most basic, mindless work and that's all. It's best to get these issues out in the open during the initial interview—ask the organization to do the same—rather than run into differing expectations in the future.

To find out about volunteer opportunities in your area, check out these online resources:

www.VolunteerMatch.org
www.Idealist.org
www.BeTheChange.org
www.211.org (United Way)
www.give.org

Don't forget that many out-of-pocket expenses you incur while volunteering, including transportation and mileage, are tax-deductible. See *IRS Publication 526 Charitable Contributions* for all the rules and regs. And why not double down, as I like to do, and donate your tax savings back to the groups you volunteered with, since you've already paid for the expenses up front?

Five Things to Fall in Love With

If you can choose your passions or at least some of them, here are a few that will help you skip some major Money Steps down the line. These life-crafts, as I call them, are worth making a conscious effort to master and enjoy. Life-crafts are the skills you need every day, the things that if you can't do for yourself, you'll end up paying someone else to do for you. But for the blessed frugal, these are not chores but favorite hobbies, acquired tastes perhaps but tastes well worth acquiring if you can.

- **Culinary arts:** Think of cooking as more of an art—something to be creative with, something with no right or wrong answers—than a science, and I bet you'll enjoy it a heck of a lot more. If you like to eat, there's no reason you shouldn't like to cook. After all, who knows your taste buds better than you? By learning and loving to cook, you'll save bushels of clams (not to mention loaves of bread and wads of dough) on pricey restaurant meals and prepared foods over the course of your lifetime. Get the whole family involved by team cooking a special meal once a week to pair with family video night; for example, cook up a steaming dish of moussaka to eat while watching *My Big Fat Greek Wedding* or a plateful of fried green tomatoes to enjoy while—well, you get the idea.

- **Needling the fashionistas:** I admire people who make their own clothing more than any other sect of do-it-yourselfers. That's not only because of their skills with needle and thread, but even more so because they have the self-confidence to stand up to the $330 billion U.S. fashion industry and say, "Stick your attitude straight up your bobbin!" The fact that the fashion industry trades and thrives on our vanities and insecurities is fabled, literally. We all learned the story "The Emperor's New Clothes" in grade school, but apparently most people thought it was about a king who liked showing off his crown jewels in public. Whenever somebody tells me she made the outfit she's wearing, I know I'm talking to a really special, beautiful person, regardless of how she

looks, someone who's self-confident enough to wear her
pride on their sleeve.

- **Popular mechanics:** Where does the water go when you
flush the toilet, and where does the new water come
from? Is it the same water, minus the toilet oysters? Is it
true that you can drink the water in the toilet tank in
case of an emergency, and how thirsty would you need
to be before you did it? When I was a kid, these were
but a few of the metaphysical mysteries that roiled my
young mind. Like most kids, I had endless curiosity
when it came to how things worked and how things
were made. But unlike most people I know, I never
really lost that curiosity, and as a result, I grew up to be
a jack-of-all-trades when it comes to tackling home
improvement projects and other repairs like those I
discuss in Chapter 3. Indulge your childhood curiosities
throughout life, and you'll develop the skills and
knowledge to save yourself some major jack. (Plus, you'll
also know that in case of an emergency you can indeed
safely drink the water in your toilet tank, although I've
never determined just what would qualify as a sufficient
"emergency.")

- **Soil sports:** Whether it's growing your own fruits and
vegetables, landscaping your yard, or just growing some
snapdragons for a dinner table bouquet, few activities
nurture more primordial satisfaction than what I call the
soil sports. In fact Americans are gravitating to
gardening in record numbers—and with record green
sprouting from our wallets. We now spend more than
forty billion dollars annually on our residential lawns
and gardens, a 300-plus percent increase over the past
twenty years. While the soil sports can have a positive
impact on your finances by saving you money on your

grocery bill and yard care costs—not to mention landscaping that increases the value of your home—be sure to control your spending, not just your crabgrass. I'm a big fan of what Miser Adviser Antonia B. dubs guerrilla gardening, refusing to pay for plant material by propagating your own (borrow a copy of *American Horticultural Society Plant Propagation* or another book on the subject from the library to learn how), swapping plant starts with fellow gardeners, and befriending local landscapers, who routinely discard plants they uproot from landscaping jobs.

- **Arts and crafts:** This plethora of pastimes, from the classic art of oil painting to crafts du jour like scrapbooking, can inspire the Renaissance Miser within and save you some serious scratch on gifts for others and decorations for your home. Lack talent or self-confidence? The belief that there's a correlation between cost and aesthetics (i.e., cheap=ugly / tasteless, expensive=beauty / tasteful) may be deeply rooted in the American psyche, but refreshingly that's not the case in many other cultures. I've been struck by this difference when I've traveled in rural and impoverished areas in other countries and seen the simplest but most exquisite, joyous display of beauty in the poorest surroundings: a brilliant pink bougainvillea vine growing proudly out of a rusty Nescafé can on a front step; a colorful self-painted mural shouting for attention on the side wall of a crumbling one-room house with a thatched roof. Good value and good taste are not mutually exclusive. Fine art is the art *you* think is fine.

101 Free or Very Frugal Things to Do

Looking for a hobby that won't hobble your bank account? Or maybe just some free fun to fill an afternoon? Check out these cheap thrills:

- **Autograph collecting** (http://ehampton.tripod.com/)
- **Birding** (www.birding.com)
- **Bottle hunting:** What? Wine used to come in bottles? (www.findmall.com/list.php?46)
- **Bug collecting** (www.entomologyclub.ifas.edu)
- **Calling—birds** (www.oldbird.org)
- **Calling—hogs** (www.porkopolis.org)
- **Calling—names:** Call me cheap, just don't call me collect. (www.nonamecallingweek.org)
- **Cartooning** (www.cartoon.org)
- **Climbing—Money Steps / NOT!** (www.UltimateCheapskate.com)
- **Climbing—stairs** (www.skyscraperchallenge.org)
- **Climbing—trees** (www.treeclimbercoalition.org)
- **Cloud gazing** (www.cloudgazing.com)
- **Composting:** Repeat after me: "A rind is a terrible thing to waste." (www.howtocompost.org)
- **Conservation** (www.nature.org)
- **Crafts—cardboard** (www.familycrafts.about.com)
- **Crafts—paper bags** (www.dhk-kids.com)
- **Crafts—scrap lumber** (www.kinderart.com)
- **Dancing** (www.danceusa.org)
- **Dream interpretation:** "Aunt Nadine? What are *you* doing here again?" (www.dreamnetwork.net)
- **Dumpster diving** (www.allthingsfrugal.com)

- **Egg tossing** (www.boredgourd.com/activity/279/egg-toss.html)
- **Fish watching:** Even more exciting than it sounds. (www.dnr.wi.gov)
- **Foraging** (www.foraging.com)
- **Fossil hunting** (geology.er.usgs.gov/eastern/fossils.html)
- **Foreign language:** Parlez-vous cheapskate? (www.foreignlanguages.com)
- **Free attractions and events** (www.free-attractions.com)
- **Free factory tours** (www.factorytourusa.com)
- **Free high school concerts** (www.schoolbands.com)
- **Frisbee golf** (www.disclife.com)
- **Genealogy** (www.genealogy.com)
- **Ghost hunting** (www.prairieghosts.com)
- **Giving a compliment** (www.complimentday.com)
- **Gravestone rubbing:** Warning: May result in chafing if attempted in the nude. (www.justcallbob.com)
- **Gurning:** What? (www.cumbria.uk.com/cumbria/fun/gurner.htm)
- **Haircutting:** At home, yours and others. (www.stretcher.com/stories/04/04mar15f.cfm)
- **Hiking** (www.americanhiking.org)
- **Ice carving** (www.nica.org)
- **Jump roping** (www.usajrf.org)
- **Kissing—oral** (www.goaskalice.columbia.edu/0903.html)
- **Kissing—other** (www.sexual-health-resource.org/oral_sex.htm)
- **Kite—building** (www.kitebuilder.com)
- **Kite—flying** (www.aka.kite.org)
- **Laughing** (www.laughbreak.com)
- **Letter writing:** The lost art of. (www.readwritethink.org)
- **Listening** (www.studygs.net)

- **Mall walking**
  (www.grandtimes.com/Tips_For_Mall.html)
- **Meditating** (www.how-to-meditate.org)
- **Massage** (www.messagenetwork.com)
- **Moss Gardening:** Perfect pastime for anyone who's not a Rolling Stone. (www.mossacres.com)
- **Mushroom hunting**
  (www.morelmushroomhunting.com)
- **Napping** (www.napping.com)
- **Naturism:** Not recommended for anyone interested in any of the following: ice sculpting, gravestone rubbing, noodling, tree sitting, whittling. (www.netnude.com)
- **Noodling:** What? (Part II) (www.okienoodling.com)
- **Orienteering** (www.us.orienteering.org)
- **Origami:** Get your mind out of the gutter. It's the art of paper folding, not something involving your neighbors and a hot tub. (www.origami.com)
- **Painting—face** (www.facepaintdesigns.co.uk)
- **Painting—finger** (www.ehow.com)
- **Painting—general** (www.painting.about.com)
- **Painting—whole body:** Send photos of your work to CheapThrills4Me@aol.com. (www.bodypainting.co.uk)
- **Pantomime** (www.pantomime.org.uk)
- **Paper airplanes** (www.paperairplanes.co.uk)
- **Papier-mâché** (www.papiermache.co.uk/)
- **Peeping—leaves** (www.foliagenetwork.com)
- **Peeping—other:** PLEASE don't look.
  (www.fun.from.hell.pl/2003-02-18/peeping.swf)
- **Pitching pennies:** And other frugal fun pastimes from yesteryears.
  (www.myrecollection.com/christianog/games.html)
- **Plaster casting—body parts** (www.bnglifecasting.com)
- **Puppets—shadow** (www.mindbluff.com)

- **Puppets—politicians** (www.funnypolitics.com)
- **Puppets—sock** (www.legendsandlove.com)
- **Reading—books:** At the library, of course. (www.travelinlibrarian.info)
- **Reading—palms** (www.handanalysis.com)
- **Reading—rear ends:** a.k.a. "Rumpology." Why are the weird Web sites always British? (www.pleasantenglish.com/html/english/personalitybuttocks.htm)
- **Recycling** (www.nrc-recycle.org)
- **Rock, paper, scissors** (www.worldrps.com)
- **Rockhounding** (www.rockhounds.com)
- **Saying "thank you"** (www.newwork.com)
- **Saying "thank you"—after sex** (www.politesex.com)
- **Sex** (www.solotouch.com)
- **Sex—with someone else** (www.tantra.com)
- **Sharing** (www.strength.org)
- **Signing** (www.handspeak.com)
- **Singing:** Like a lark. Which, BTW, you can shoot out of season (not really). (www.choral.org)
- **Sketching** (www.picturedraw.co.uk)
- **Stretching** (www.stretchingusa.com)
- **Stargazing:** Is that the Big Dipper, or are you just happy to see me? (www.stargate.org)
- **Telling—jokes** (www.humor.about.com)
- **Telling—other people off** (www.insult-o-matic.com)
- **Telling—stories** (www.storyarts.org)
- **Tai chi** (www.easytaichi.com)
- **Tree sitting** (www.answers.com/topic/tree-sitting)
- **UFO spotting:** Great hobby to combine with tree sitting. (www.rense.com)
- **Ventriloquism** (www.ventriloquism101.com)
- **Walking** (www.thewalkingsite.com)

- **Whistling:** While you skip the Money Steps. (www.wannalearn.com)
- **Whittling** (www.whittling.com)
- **Writing—fiction** (www.fictionwriting.about.com)
- **Writing—general** (www.oregon.state.edu)
- **Writing—poetry** (www.poetrymajic.co.uk)
- **Yodeling:** You'll be a hit at any party, at least if it's a party attended by fish watchers or moss gardeners. (www.yodelcourse.com)
- **Yoga** (www.yogabasics.com)

Travel, with a Capital T

You can imagine that I, being a cheapskate, grimace at the mere mention of taking a vacation. You bet I do. My wallet anxiety immediately flares up when I hear talk of $250-a-night resorts, lying on a beach and sipping $10 umbrella drinks, and hotel minibars with $18 jars of macadamia nuts. Let's just say that a Speedo doesn't do my tightwad justice.

But I'm frequently accused of being a cheap-*fake* when the conversation turns to places I've been and things I've seen. To quote my favorite Johnny Cash song, "I've been everywhere, man, I've been everywhere." Well, not really, but more places than most. And certainly more places than you'd expect of a spending-challenged guy like me.

You see, I believe that Travel—with a capital *T*—is not a luxury but a responsibility. I don't know why we were put here on this earth or if there even is a reason (and let's be honest, neither do you), but one thing's for sure: There are lots of other people and places out there. How can meeting them, seeing them, knowing them, appreciating them, be anything other than a responsibility, an obligation of our mutual existence, no matter what you believe?

Travel, as opposed to vacation, is yet another thing that's best done on the cheap. The smaller the Money Step, the more genuine the Travel experience. Spend a lot of money on luxury travel (or, worst of all, take a package or group tour), and you defeat the whole purpose of Traveling in the first place. You'll end up ensconced in a top-dollar Americanized hotel, eating meals identical to those you eat back home, and meeting only fellow travelers just like yourself, those who are afraid to actually get out and experience the place and meet the people who live there.

Some tips for Traveling, with a capital *T,* the cheapskate way:

- **Guidebooks kill.** By all means read up on the places you'll be visiting and use a good guidebook (I like the *Lonely Planet* series; www.LonelyPlanet.com) to get a sense of the place, its history, and logistics, but don't use it as a script for your trip. Guidebooks, even the most unpopular ones, direct huge numbers of travelers to the restaurants, hotels, and attractions they recommend, so much so that once a place is featured it's usually no longer the kind of place a real Traveler wants to go. You won't find a genuine, local experience there, and you'll undoubtedly pay a lot more.
- **Travel without reservations.** This is a point of contention when I travel with my wife, who used to have a panic attack at the very thought of traveling without any hotel reservations. But she's gradually coming around, and now we usually agree that the only hotel reservation we'll make when traveling overseas is for the first night when we arrive, for both Denise's peace of mind and jet lag relief. Otherwise we'll wing it. Not only do advance reservations cut off your ability to follow your nose, but

the places you can reserve from far away usually charge a premium and are not the kinds of places that real Travelers find satisfying.

- **A shorter distance gets you further.** travelers (those with a lowercase *t)* brag about how much ground they cover and how many different places they visit during their trips, while Travelers revel in just the opposite. To travel slowly, covering short distances and staying places longer, is to really get a sense of place and people. And once again, it's generally much more economical than rushing from one tourist trap to the next must-see destination.

- **Local transportation is best.** Particularly if you limit the distances you plan to cover, making your way as the locals do—by bus, train, ferry, foot, and even bicycle—is the best way to meet people and save some major dinero. Since folks in other countries are much more dependent on public transportation than we Americans, you'll be surprised at how user friendly and efficient most of these transport systems are, even in less developed areas. TIP: When you plan to stay in a place for more than a couple of days, pick up a used bicycle at a secondhand store, and use it for sightseeing and local transportation. You can probably even sell it back to the store at the end of your visit.

- **The three L's rule: Look for a line of locals.** Looking for a great meal or a friendly beer in a place you've never been before? Put away your guidebook, and open your eyes. No matter where you go, the best restaurant critics are the folks who live, eat, and drink there every day.

- **Hostels—not just for kids anymore.** In the interest of full disclosure, I worked for Hostelling International—USA (www.HIUSA.org) for many years, and among other wonderful things I owe to that fine organization, I met my wife through hosteling. In short, *real* Travelers stay at hostels. Hostelling International is the organization behind nearly four thousand hostels in more than sixty countries worldwide. Forget what you think you know about hostels. They're not just for young people anymore; people of all ages are welcome, and senior Travelers are a burgeoning clientele. Hostels are not flophouses; they're safe, clean, comfortable, and yes, very, very, very affordable (try twenty to thirty dollars a night in major cities like Paris, London, and New York; lesser locations cost much less, of course). Most of all, hostels are *the* place to meet local folks and fellow Travelers, kindred spirits who are talking versions of what you hope to find in a guidebook but never do.

I read once that fear (of others, the unknown, etc.) is overcome by understanding. Understanding leads to appreciation, appreciation leads to love, and love leads to peace. That's why Travel, with a capital *T,* is a responsibility, not a luxury.

9

Getting Your Nest Egg Laid

How to read a prospectus: Start at the beginning, usually page 1. As soon as you come to the part about "past performance is no indication of future results," stop reading. Have you ever noticed that even lottery tickets aren't required to say anything that ominous?

—the Ultimate Cheapskate on investing

I went to the bank and reviewed my savings. I found out I have all the money I'll ever need. If I die tomorrow.

—Henny Youngman

As you know all too well by now, the purpose of this book is to provide advice about spending less and enjoying life more, *not* about making (and spending) more money. If you were expecting the latter—perhaps another fictional read about getting rich overnight—you probably stopped reading two hundred pages ago.

However, contrary to what some might think, I'm not opposed to having money. As Woody Allen once said, "Money is better than poverty, if only for financial reasons." For the most part I feel ambivalent about having more money versus having less, just so long as I have "enough," as discussed earlier. Beyond enough, what's the point?

I could truly take it as well as I could leave it, or at the very least I don't spend appreciable time thinking about it either way. Occasionally things I do make money (like writing this book, for example), and other times they don't (like training for an entire month to see how many deviled eggs I can eat at the family reunion—seventy-seven halves, top that!), but money is no longer my motivation for deciding what I do or don't do. And that's the primary point of this book.

All that having been said, many people I've spoken with while I've been writing this book have urged me to include at least one chapter that briefly discusses my philosophy for the revenue side of the equation, specifically for investing. I'm extremely hesitant to do so, as I don't want readers to lose sight of my true message—SPEND LESS MONEY!—and very important (so listen carefully), I've never professed to have particularly strong skills or expertise in the field of investing. My expertise is in the nonprofit sector, which thrives on doing the most with the least, so I'm happy to let others with more expertise provide investing and other moneymaking advice, if you're into that sort of thing.

But with some trepidation I bow to my advisers and offer a few final observations about nest eggs.

Putting Your Portfolio in Perspective

If you've ever scrolled down through the list of personal finance books available on Amazon.com, you'll notice that the vast majority (approximately 80 percent, by my count) deal primarily, if not exclusively, with the revenue side of personal finance. In short, they offer advice for managing your portfolio or otherwise maximizing income / assets. I find that curious, because in my own Hierarchy of Moolah Management the traditional portfolio is a pretty small, relatively unimportant part of the mix.

Here's how I prioritize things in my Hierarchy of Moolah Management, from the most to the least important:

1. **Reduce your dependency on money as much as possible.** To repeat an earlier paraphrase, "A penny saved is a penny you don't need to earn." Skip or reduce the Money Steps. If you doubt me further about the priority I place on this simple strategy, certainly you've heard about very wealthy people who have lost everything. How do you suppose that happens? Could it be that they spent / risked too much?

There are two parts to this one:

    a. Reduce your ongoing spending, and thereby decrease cash flow needs.

    b. Eliminate all debt, saving interest charges and greatly reducing the possibility of nasty things like foreclosure, bankruptcy, etc.

2. **Maintain your health, thereby preserving your ability to earn money as needed and reducing the chances of incurring catastrophic medical expenses.** Remember, for most people their greatest asset isn't their houses or their investments. It's their ability to earn money, and that depends directly on their maintaining good health.

3. **Safeguard your assets, both liquid and fixed.** There are three elements to address:

    a. Develop a proclivity for safe(r) investments.

    b. Create an individualized asset allocation plan, a plan for what types of investment makes sense for you, on the basis of your feelings about risk and your financial goals. I'll tell you about mine shortly, as an example.

    c. Maintain appropriate insurance.

4. **Attempt to maximize the growth of your portfolio, as time and interest allow (optional).**

While we could debate the rank of some of these items (particularly 1 and 2, which I would rank as such only in an economic context, never in a quality of life context), once you've slain your *Enoughasaurus* it's clear that maximizing the growth of your portfolio is the lowest priority. Once you've determined what's enough for you, you've set a fixed point, and the other considerations take precedence.

I'm at a loss to explain why so many people myopically focus on their portfolios as the most important aspect of their finances—other than, of course, the obvious sexual magnetism of Suze Orman and some of the other personal finance gurus who preach this fiscal philosophy. In fact, whenever I see Suze Orman on TV, I think there must be something wrong with me. If only I could have the kind of toe-curling Orman-gasm Suze has every time she talks about her portfolio. But no, I am but a simple cheapskate and must settle for free, old-fashioned sex.

OBSERVATION 1: Focusing on your portfolio as the most important aspect of your financial life is definitely the best course of action, just so long as you're the kind of person who is instantly aroused by Suze Orman. Otherwise, put your portfolio in perspective, and get a real life.

If Only Equities Were More Equitable

The problem with investing in stocks is that in order to be really successful at it, you must act the exact opposite of human nature. And that's incredibly difficult. The old but so true adage

"Buy low, sell high" is like willing yourself to stop in the middle of an orgasm, only harder. You need to sell your stock on the day that you feel best about owning it, and you need to buy more stock on the day that you feel worst about owning any in the first place.

As if that weren't impossible enough, *all the time* you need to disregard what everyone who claims to be a stock expert is telling you, and to do so in reverse proportion to how much you're paying him or her. In other words, the people collecting the highest fees from you should be ignored the most. Someone professing to have no expertise in the field and offering free advice (e.g., anyone named after an animal like Moose or Possum whom you meet in a bar, particularly if he's wearing a T-shirt that says something like "Who Farted?") is probably the best source of counsel if you feel the need for outside advice.

If you question my opinion on this point, just look at what the "experts" were saying on the eve of the tech stock collapse in 2000. I recall reading after that financial meltdown that at the time less than 10 percent of financial advisors were counseling their clients to sell the shares that were about to take a nosedive. All other financial oracles were still advising "hold," "buy," or even "strong buy." I'll take my chances with the Ouija board anytime.

In all seriousness, investing in stocks for the long term is a pretty good strategy, in my opinion, and as you'll see in a minute, stocks make up about 60 percent of the Yeagers' nest egg (not including the value of our home). Even then it's still likely to require you to act contrary to human nature at various points in your investing lifetime, and I'm not joking about the difficulty of doing that when the time comes.

If you question my opinion on this point, again just look at what happened during the tech stock run-up of the late 1990s. Millions of Americans who intended to pull money out of the stock market in order to retire got, in a word, *greedy* and stayed in too long. As a result, many are still punching the clock and probably punching holes in the living room wall as well. Nonetheless, the buy and hold approach at least minimizes the number of times you must will yourself to stop in the middle of your ecstasy, and (only) when it comes to stock investing, that's a good thing.

Generally the simplest and cheapest, and therefore I say the *best*, way of doing this is to buy index funds, funds that are designed to mimic the performance of an underlying index, like Standard & Poor's 500. Because concocting these investment mixtures is more a matter of mathematics than financial wisdom, the fees you pay for fund management are generally much lower than "actively managed" funds. Plus, since index funds trade less frequently, they frequently produce lower capital gains distributions.

OBSERVATION 2: Investing in stocks is definitely the best course of action, just so long as you're the kind of person who can will him / herself to stop in the middle of an orgasm. Otherwise, buy index funds and diversify.

Small Cap? Mid-Cap? Large Cap? I Say MAD CAP!

Most financial advisors caution typical investors like you and me against investing in individual stocks of our own choosing, opting instead for mutual funds and other investment products managed by investing "pros." Despite my rather low opinion of most of these pros and my proclivity for index funds and other passively managed funds over the more exotic, costly, actively managed funds, I do support the conclusion that mutual funds should constitute most of the equity portion of your portfolio. It's as simple as not putting all your eggs in one basket, and mutual funds are a convenient way of weaving those baskets.

Nonetheless, I strongly encourage everyone who has even a modest portfolio to set aside some portion—I suggest 5 percent of the total—as his own "Mad Cap Fund." That is money you use to invest in the individual stocks that appeal to you. Now that you can easily and inexpensively buy and sell stocks online, the costs associated with creating your own Mad Cap Fund are minimal, just so long as you don't trade too often.

How should you decide what stocks to buy? How the hell should I know? Maybe you're the studious type and you'll analyze companies' financial statements, annual reports, and other corporate documents, or maybe you have a friend who whispers sweet stock tips in your ear. Maybe you'll throw darts at the stock page, or use my old-fashioned favorite and simply choose companies that impress you as a consumer. After all, you're as good a consumer as the next guy—maybe even better, since you're reading this book.

With luck your Mad Cap Fund will perform well, and you'll get a decent return. Even if it doesn't, your exposure is limited. Creating a Mad Cap Fund is not so much an intelligent investment as it is an investment in your intelligence. It's a way of realizing new financial appreciation, in both senses of the word. It's a way of increasing your knowledge and maintaining a healthy interest in the investing side of personal finance, and at the same time it provides a cathartic release for those who might otherwise be tempted to "overmanage" their own portfolios.

One word of optimistic caution, though: On the basis of my prediction that your Mad Cap Fund may in fact do better than other portions of your portfolio, periodic rebalancing is extremely important. I suggest that once a year on a set anniversary date (might I propose April Fool's Day, as you'll be one if you don't take this advice?) you rebalance your Mad Cap Fund to ensure that it remains approximately 5 percent of your total portfolio. If that means needing to put more money into it, that decision is up to you. But if your Mad Cap Fund has outperformed other components of your portfolio, bite the bullet, and draw it back down to the 5 percent level.

This may hurt—I know, "It's the best horse on the track!"—but your Mad Cap Fund is likely to be weighted heavily in a few favorite stocks and therefore subject to extreme volatility. To ease your anxiety, try setting up a special money market account as I have for the money you take off the table. That way you'll have the satisfaction of being able to see the rewards of your savvy investing, while safeguarding the earnings and providing a ready pot of money to replenish your Mad Cap Fund if needed. If the pot grows large enough, you can then reinvest it proportionately across your portfolio or take it out and spend it as truly mad money.

Bonds: Better Bored than Broke

If investing in stocks is like coitus interruptus, then investing in bonds is like holy matrimony (forgive me, honey, I'm referring to other people's marriages, not ours)—very comfortable, very familiar, rewarding and enjoyable enough—but the challenge is keeping it interesting so that you don't go looking for something more exciting. Bonds and other lending investments—investments where your money is a loan to a company or other entity, as opposed to stocks where you're becoming part owner by purchasing equity—are usually safe(r) alternatives to stocks.

The challenge of successfully investing in bonds and other lending investments like certificates of deposit, treasury bills, and money market / savings accounts is largely a matter of patience. In exchange for far greater security than you typically have with stocks or other riskier investments, the price you pay with lending investments is sheer boredom and frequent frustration over the lower returns that you're likely to receive in the long run.

With lending investments it's more often a matter of resisting action than taking action, at least once you've set your basic investments in motion. When you see others raking in the dough during stock market rallies, it's easy to forget about all the restful nights you've enjoyed during slumps in the market and to decide to cash out of your boring lending investments. But when that urge strikes you, remember my observation about the difficulty of buying low / selling high: Whenever you're most enthusiastic about stocks, that's probably _not_ the time to buy.

Despite the ho-hum factor, I agree with the conventional wisdom about using lending investments to help diversify your portfolio according to your individualized asset allocation plan. Not only should that plan take into consideration your age, investment goals, and risk tolerance, but with regard to lending investments, you might want to beef up that portion of your portfolio even more if you have a greater need for current income (as opposed to long-term growth) or if you really need the tax benefits provided by municipal bonds. In our case, as you'll see in a minute, about a third of the Ultimate Cheapskate's total portfolio is in lending investments, perhaps somewhat more than typical for people our age, but this reflects our potential need to draw current income.

Like with stocks, I prefer investing in bonds via mutual funds for the convenience and diversification. Also, to keep your options more flexible and to provide a little more spark in your lending investment love life, always "ladder" your CDs and treasury bills (i.e., use different maturity dates) whenever possible.

OBSERVATION 3: Investing only in bonds and fixed rate of return investments is definitely the best course of action, just so long as you're the kind of person who has never fantasized about anyone other than your spouse. Otherwise, diversify and take a cold shower.

Trimming Your Personal Finance Payroll

One of the most astute financial observations I've ever heard came from my nephew Stephen, who was eleven at the time. He overheard me mentioning something about needing to call my broker for money advice. "But, Uncle Jeff," he said innocently, "why do you want to call someone who's broker for advice about making money?" From the mouths of babes . . .

Having served on nonprofit boards and run organizations that oversaw what, at least for them, were significant endowments, I can honestly say that the decision to hire outside financial advisors to help manage those funds was made with one overriding consideration in mind: CYA (that's cover your ass, *not* competitive yield analysis).

With all due respect to the investment companies and individuals we worked with, in the nonprofit sector we felt a tremendous responsibility to exhibit proper stewardship of those endowment funds. The endowments were usually donated money and the lifeblood of the organizations they supported.

While individual investors don't have exactly the same outside considerations, I think many will admit to feeling a similar desire to CYA. Most people want someone else to be responsible if things go wrong. Enter financial advisors, planners, fund managers, brokers, and a host of other professional money gurus. As Jean-Paul Sartre reasoned, "in deciding once, we have decided all," or "in not deciding, we have decided," or something like that.

Being the Ultimate Cheapskate, I'm understandably reluctant to pay anyone to do anything for me. That's doubly true when it comes to paying someone to manage my money. It's not just about the fees; it's about the quality and objectivity of the advice you're likely to receive.

Many financial advisors are paid commissions on the investment "products" they sell their clients, creating what seems to me to be an inherent conflict of interest on their part. Simply, they can make higher commissions by selling you certain investments instead of others and by convincing you to frequently buy / sell investments (aka churning your account), with each transaction generating more commissions for the advisor. What's more, beyond their thinly veiled sales pitches, commission-based advisors have no incentive, and rarely much expertise, when it comes to providing other personal financial advice (e.g., the pros and cons of paying down your mortgage versus buying an investment property).

And while fee-only advisors (i.e., those who charge by the hour or a flat fee—no commissions) may have something of value to offer some clients, finding a decent one is extremely difficult. The fee-only advisors I've encountered seem mostly interested in selling you a one-size-fits-all plan or racking up big-time hourly fees by telling you stuff you already know. Again, this approach is probably a wise financial one—for the advisor. Nonetheless, hiring a fee-only advisor for a few hours to double-check the financial plan you put together on your own may provide a sense of CYA, which some investors might decide is worth the price.

As discussed elsewhere, I'm also happy to purge traditional brokers from my personal finance payroll. I now much prefer to do my own (albeit limited) trading online, where I can both reduce my fees and eliminate the BS hassle (that's bullshit, *not buy / sell*) that you get with most "live" brokers.

On the rare, almost unheard of, occasions when I invest in a higher-fee "actively managed" mutual fund, you can bet that those fund managers are going to lose my business if they don't consistently outperform the fund's benchmark by enough to make it worth my while and justify their fees, particularly since you can usually buy index funds—with absolute minimal fees—that will match the performance of the indexes commonly used as benchmarks. The old saying "Results, not excuses" is the ultimate benchmark when it comes to holding high-priced mutual fund managers responsible for superior performance.

Depending on the complexity of your finances, you may need to hire a qualified accountant and tax attorney to help manage your affairs. You have my blessing. Those are professionals with technical expertise and training that I respect. Plus, they charge by the hour and, very important, assume some degree of liability should their advice prove incorrect. For all those reasons, I have no qualms about paying those folks a reasonable fee if your situation warrants.

Now, I'm not saying that *absolutely* everyone is capable of managing his own finances all the time. What I'm saying is that no one—even a "professional"—is *absolutely* capable of managing his own finances all the time. There's always a degree of risk and uncertainty, and with the exceptions noted above, I'm not convinced there's a significant correlation between paying fees and either reducing risks or increasing returns.

If you apply yourself and make a modest investment of time

and effort, commodities you can afford if you're not busy earning the money to pay someone else for *his* time and effort, I predict you'll do a better job than anyone you're likely to hire. After all, you have a vested interest in the outcome, and so much of successful investing is a matter of understanding your individual situation, needs, goals, and attitude toward things like risk tolerance. No, my advice for managing your own finances is much the same as my advice for doing your own plumbing: Go for it, but remember that even the best plumbers—and financial managers—occasionally have some crappy results.

OBSERVATION 4: Relying on a qualified financial advisor to manage all your money is definitely the best course of action, just so long as you're the kind of person who has never pleasured himself before. Otherwise, you know that sometimes you can do the job yourself.

MATH CONFUSION: Fees—Fie, Foe, Fum

Maybe it's just a sad testament to the intellectual capacity of the folks I hang around with, but I've spent more than one long evening trying to convince my sorry cohorts that they're gravely mistaken when they dismiss as "trivial" the sales and operating fees they're paying for their mutual funds and other investments.

I don't mean to give the impression that we spend a lot of time sitting around discussing money. In fact we probably spend as much time discussing Paris Hilton as we spend discussing money, which is to say very little, but ashamedly some. And compared with the hours we spend yakking about other world events, like the reasons behind the demise of socialism or whether Takeru Kobayashi will smash the fifty-five hot dog barrier in next year's Nathan's

Famous Hot Dog Eating Contest, the time we spend on money /
Paris truly is trivial.

"Hell, it's only 4 percent! You know, Yeager, you're supposed to
tip at least 15, even 20 percent to a freaking waiter!" This statement epitomizes another cataclysmic case of math confusion.

This one is pretty simple, although apparently not as simple as
my friends. The sales and annual operating fees you're probably
paying on your mutual funds and other investment accounts (as
well as for commission and fee-based financial advisors) are, almost without exception, based on a percentage of the total value
of your funds. They're not taking a cut of what you actually earn in
a given year or the loss you might take. The fees get paid, regardless.

Say Paris Hilton invests $100,000 in a mutual fund. *(Oh, that's
so hot!)* Commissions (aka sales loads) and operating expenses for
the year total 4.5 percent, but the fund has a total return of say
$9,000, or 9 percent, for the year. *(Now that's hot!)* Paris is proba-
bly feeling pretty cheeky about getting away with "tipping" only
4.5 percent. *(Daddy says tipping is so hot!)* Wait a minute. That
4.5 percent ($4,500) is actually *50* percent—a full half—of what
Paris made from the fund for the year. *(Even Daddy's not that big
a tipper!)* Look at it from another perspective: What investor
wouldn't jump at a chance to increase his return by 50 percent?

Now it's almost impossible to invest with any diversity and not
incur at least some fees. But in my opinion, higher fees (including
any sales loads or annual operating expenses of more than 1 percent for stock funds or more than 0.5 percent for bond funds) are
never justified. You can find plenty of terrific funds that meet these
criteria. Study after study has shown that load funds don't perform
better than no-load funds (in fact overall their performance is
worse), even before the increased costs are factored in.

Research also shows that for periods over ten or more years,
simple index funds (which usually have the lowest fees of all) out-

perform actively managed funds three-quarters of the time. Even if you're inclined to take the sucker's bet and think you can pick the 25 percent winning ticket, do you really believe you can do it for each of the mutual funds you probably own? Those odds, not to mention significantly lower fees and generally reduced capital gains, keep me coming back to index funds, as discussed previously.

So, by failing to appreciate the difference between a percentage of gross versus a percentage of net, many investors shrug off investment / management fees as inconsequential when they're clearly one of the most important considerations once you've cut through the math confusion.

I'll Show You Mine . . .

OK, so with the same sense of queasy anxiety I had the first time I dropped my shorts in the boys' locker room as Coach Sacstretcher looked on with amusement, here goes!

At the time of writing this book, I would estimate the net worth of my wife and me to be approximately $900,000. That includes an educated self-estimate of the current market value of our house (approximately $450,000), which we own free and clear, and about $50,000 in other real property—cars, furniture, my fake vomit collection, etc. The remaining $400,000 or so is in a variety of retirement accounts and other short- and long-term investments. Throughout this book I discuss how we've amassed our savings on relatively modest salaries (hint: SPEND LESS MONEY!), but here I want to address how we manage and invest those savings.

First, a reminder that I'm sharing this information about our portfolio *not* as a model for your own but rather as a real-life example of how reasonably intelligent people can make reasonable decisions about their own portfolios with a reasonable investment of time and effort. Many aspects of investing are highly individualized, so when it comes to plans for managing your wealth, one size doesn't fit all, even though that's what many professional financial planners are peddling. And other factors like risk tolerance are entirely subjective, with no right or wrong answers. So I hope that after I've shown you mine, you'll spend a little time thinking about your own portfolio—with or without the help of an outside "expert"—since your involvement in the process is essential.

Like a lot of folks who have had multiple employers during their careers, our retirement accounts appear, on the surface, to be a confusing mess of many different funds with several different financial institutions. Every time one of us started a new job, we started a new retirement account, which inevitably consisted of a variety of funds. A few years ago I resolved to tidy things up, to review our portfolio and consolidate our holdings through a single institution. But after a weekend of digging into the details of the gigantic jumble, I came to the conclusion that through some quirk of fiduciary evolution (clearly *not* intelligent design), our curious collection of retirement investments was just about perfect for us at that time.

When I looked beyond the mere number of accounts and closely examined the types and compositions of the individual funds, I found that our retirement investments (i.e., those in 401(k) and other accounts that penalize you for withdrawal prior to traditional retirement ages—in our case about $220,000 of our total nest egg) consisted of about 85 percent stocks and 15 percent bonds and other nonstock investments. I'm sure some experts would say that this mix relies too heavily on stocks. The general rule of thumb is to subtract your current age from 100 (some say 110), and the remainder is the percentage you should have in stocks. In our case, that would have been 55 to 60 percent at the time. But when factoring in our nonretirement savings, not to mention the equity in our entirely paid-for home, I think the stock component seems very reasonable, even conservative.

Then I really waded into the weeds, looking at each individual fund, its objectives, its historical performance, and some of its largest holdings. My goal was to see how much overlap existed among various funds in our total portfolio. I made a simple spreadsheet (cleverly using a piece of paper, silly, not some specialized computer software) to keep track of my findings as I plowed through the stack of quarterly statements provided by the different investment firms.

First I categorized each fund by type and then classified the types according to low, medium, or high risk. Then, on the basis of the current value of each fund, I calculated the percentage each fund represented of the total.

Again, what emerged out of this apparent chaos was a picture that seemed reasonable to me and palatable in terms of risk, despite an admitted lack of planning. Approximately 50 percent of our stock investments were in my mid-risk range, 15 percent were in the low-risk range, and 35 percent I classified as high risk. Different experts would no doubt give different opinions about this approach and the mix itself, but they'd be the first to tell you that risk tolerance—that is, your comfort level with the possibility of losing money and / or experiencing dramatic fluctuations in value—is a subjective, personal issue, one without a single right answer. And while I'm not a big risk taker when it comes to money, keep in mind that our other nonretirement investments help increase my comfort level with the 35 percent of our total savings that is higher risk.

As a result of this review, I did discover a couple of funds that seemed to have a particularly poor track record when compared with the same type of funds managed by other firms already found in our portfolio. For example, an international stock fund we'd invested in for nearly ten years had a consistently dreadful performance compared with many other international stock funds.

Because I wanted to maintain international stocks as a portion of our portfolio—but I'd prefer a faster horse, thank you—I was able with a phone call to sell the poor performer and roll the proceeds into a highly regarded mid-cap fund with that same firm. With a second phone call to another institution that holds some of our retirement savings, I invested in its top-ranked international stock fund, selling an equivalent amount of our lackluster mid-cap holdings with that company to fund the investment. It was a simple, two-phone-call swap. While I don't recommend changing horses like this too often—you risk what I call fanciful financier syndrome—it does show the value of having your investments housed with a number of credible institutions, not just a single firm.

As for our nonretirement savings, these consist of various moneys we've squirreled away over the years, approximately $180,000 of our $400,000 portfolio. Because these funds aren't locked up in penalty-toting retirement accounts, we can tap them at any age, as a source of first resort if we need money. Because of this, we've tried to manage these funds to accomplish a number of different objectives: liquidity (~25 percent in savings / money market accounts), low-risk (~40 percent in CDs and short-term notes), conservative growth (~25 percent in blue chip and similar index funds), and approximately 10 percent (or 5 percent of the total $400,000 egg) in a "Mad Cap Fund," which I talked about earlier.

In addition to the above assets, as discussed in Chapter 5 we have a small attached guesthouse that we rent out, which currently generates about seven thousand dollars (gross) each year. My wife will also be entitled to some modest employer-funded pensions when she retires; these will probably be a couple of hundred dollars a month, at most. And we're both eligible to collect Social Security when we reach the qualifying age(s), provided that Social Security is still around at that time.

So there you have it, the Yeager nest egg cracked wide open for all to see, a hearty helping of huevos à la cheapskate. Certainly not the biggest one around, but as Coach Sacstretcher taught us in eighth-grade boys' health, "It's not the size of your dilly whacker; it's what you do with it!" Someone recently told me that Coach Sacstretcher left teaching and is now a successful financial advisor.

OBSERVATION 5: Portfolio envy is a lot like penis envy. Both are examples of irrationally coveting something that's probably temporarily inflated.

The Million-Dollar Mantra

So, can the Yeagers (ages forty-eight and fifty-four) afford to retire today? *Absolutely not,* according to everything I've ever read and to the financial planners and other "experts" I've spoken with over the years.

"You need at least a million dollars, *not* including the value of your house, to retire! And maybe a lot more!" they typically say.

Alas, the Million-Dollar Mantra, inevitably delivered in a tone intended to crush any hope that a mere mortal like you or me can ever achieve the end in question. And if you think you might be able to reach the million-dollar milestone, there's always the qualifier—"and maybe a lot more!"—just to keep your optimism in check.

But I question the validity of the Million-Dollar Mantra, at least as a universal truth. For example, in our case I would say that we probably can't afford to retire at this point, or at least it wouldn't be very prudent, but I wouldn't rule it out entirely. Fortunately, as I discussed earlier, we really don't want to retire now. We just want the luxury of being selfishly employed, free to pursue our passions as work, without inordinate worry about collecting a steady paycheck or unnecessary attention to amassing more money.

I think in our case it's not so much that we're so short on money (a net worth of nine hundred thousand dollars is nothing to sneeze at), as that we're just too long on years. We're still relatively young and in fairly good health, meaning we should either eat more eggs to increase our cholesterol or let our nest egg grow at least a few more years.

Even if our "selfish employment" activities generate only enough to cover our modest living expenses and our investments grow by a conservative 5 percent annually, our current four-hundred-thousand-dollar nest egg will grow to more than nine hundred thousand dollars by the time I'm sixty-five. That's within spitting distance of the Million-Dollar Mantra, for what that's worth, all without adding a single new dollar of savings to the nest. This is a tribute to the mathematical beauty of compound interest and a testament to the virtue of laying your nest egg early in life.

When you probe the underlying assumptions behind the Million-Dollar Mantra, I'm astonished at how generalized they turn out to be. It's a prime example of the one-size-fits-all approach to financial planning. In other words, it's pretty useless.

For example, whether or not your house is paid off is a relatively small consideration in many retirement income calculators that lead you to the inescapable conclusion that you need at least a million dollars in order to retire. I remember seeing one a few years ago that stated that if your home mortgage is entirely paid off, you "may" be able to budget lower annual housing costs in your retirement years. Wow, now that's financial genius! In fact I'll go out on a limb and say you "definitely" can budget lower housing costs once you're no longer paying a mortgage!

Inevitably the Million-Dollar Mantra is based on a premise that you'll need at least 80 to 90 percent (some say as much as 110 percent) of your preretirement income to live comfortably in retirement and that you should draw no more than 4.5 to 5 percent out of your nest egg annually. I think the annual draw amount is solid advice; that's the same spending policy most endowment funds operate under to avoid cannibalizing themselves over time. But basing your postretirement income needs on your preretirement income is like planning your funeral on the basis of what you did on your wedding night; no matter how hard you wish, one really doesn't have anything to do with the other.

Once, at the urging of a mutual friend, I met with a financial advisor regarding our retirement plans. It quickly frustrated me because he insisted that I compile all sorts of tax and investing documents for his review and fill out extensive questionnaires. Not that this was unreasonable or unexpected, but from the beginning I had a sneaking suspicion that his "analysis" would consist of placing the documents in a neatly labeled file folder.

I explained repeatedly during our meetings and on the questionnaires that while my wife and I were earning approximately $75,000 at the time, we were in fact spending significantly less than half of that (including house payments that would no longer be a factor by the time we retired) and that we were content to live out our remaining years at that same level, adjusting for inflation, of course. You guessed it. When his beautifully bound report was presented to me, it started with the premise that we would need an annual income of $67,500 (i.e., 90 percent of $75,000) to live comfortably in retirement. Junk in, junk out.

In fact the formulas behind the Million-Dollar Mantra invariably seem more like prescriptions for a self-fulfilling prophecy than a tool for legitimate financial planning. They appear to me to be designed to lead to the foregone conclusion that you'll need at least a million dollars to retire comfortably, regardless of your specific circumstances and expectations. In addition to trivializing "little things," like whether or not your house will be paid off by the time you retire, many of these retirement calculators downplay or entirely ignore other major considerations, such as:

- *Dependents* (pre- and postretirement): Do you currently have dependent children and / or other dependents (e.g., aged parents), and what are they costing you? What support, if any, might they continue to require of you in your retirement?
- *Health:* Obviously no one knows how long he'll live, but if you chronically suffer from poor health, you can likely expect higher health care costs in retirement. But the silver lining is that you may not live so long! To reiterate, good health means good wealth, particularly during retirement. While you may live longer, and that may require a bigger nest egg, you lower your cost of living and keep your options open when you have good health, including your ability to earn additional income if needed.
- *Health care:* Are you willing to pursue part-time employment in retirement to secure health insurance if

needed? Are you healthy enough to get insurance easily and relatively inexpensively?

- _Home equity:_ Are you willing to relocate and / or downsize your home in retirement to generate additional funds? Are you willing to take out a reverse mortgage on your home if needed?
- _Estate planning:_ How do you feel about the importance of leaving wealth to others (e.g., family, charitable organizations) upon your death? If you have heirs apparent, how do they feel about it? Not only is this essential information in terms of calculating your spendable savings, but it also impacts on decisions regarding life insurance.
- _Marital relations:_ Are you married, and if so, do you consider it a strong possibility that you will continue to be married to the same person in retirement (a postretirement divorce can cut the spending power of each spouse way down)? If not, would you like to marry during your retirement years? Would you consider remarrying if your spouse dies before you do?
- _Final wishes:_ Truly last, but not least, what provisions have you included in your living will regarding efforts to keep you alive should you become deathly ill? The more extensive the life-sustaining provisions, the more money you'd better have to pay for them.

I realize that it's impossible to answer some of these questions with absolute certainty, let alone assign specific dollar amounts, the modus operandi of most retirement savings calculators. But to ignore these mega issues entirely is clearly a gigantic shortcoming in most of these planning tools.

Because most retirement calculators provide an alphabetized

checklist of typical household expenses for you to complete, it's common for the first item on the list to be "cable TV." Now not only is that item a big fat zero dollars annually at the cable-free House of Yeager, but the fact that it is entered into the equation while other major considerations are ignored altogether reminds me of something my grandpa Tex used to say: "It's a case of not being able to see the forest because a giant sequoia just fell on top of you."

 ## We Hold These Truths to Be So Self-Evident We're Not Even Charging You for Them

Every financial planning book ever written contains the following savings / investing advice. Apparently if you recite the First Amendment backward, skipping every fourth word while playing Pink Floyd's "Money" in the background, it stipulates that freedom of the press has only one limitation—namely, that all personal finance books shall state these twelve trusted principles.

The difference is that this book includes them at no extra charge. You'll notice that this book is priced at $12.95. Why not an even $13.00 as originally planned? Because the publisher agreed that since the following pointers are so oft-repeated and self-evident, it's simply no longer fair to charge readers for them. Enjoy—our treat!

Rate Your Own Mastery of the Obvious: Circle the response that best describes your level of knowledge. KEY:

Duh: Yes, I already knew that.
Duuuh: Of course I knew that, stupid!
Duuuuuuuuh: Hell, even my senile grandmother knows that!

1. Pay yourself first. That is, religiously deposit your own savings in the appropriate account(s) before spending money on discretionary items.

Duh   Duuuh   Duuuuuuuuh

2. Start early. Although it can be hard to save money early in life, because of the mathematical beauty of compounding, even a little bit can grow into a whole lot if you sock it away early enough. Plus, establishing good savings habits when you're young makes it second nature as you grow older.

Duh   Duuuh   Duuuuuuuuh

3. Always make the maximum allowable contribution to your 401(k) or other employer-provided retirement plans, especially if the employer makes a matching contribution. This money grows tax-free until you withdraw it.

Duh   Duuuh   Duuuuuuuuh

4. Establish an individual retirement account (IRA) if your employer doesn't provide a plan or even if it does and you still qualify.

Duh   Duuuh   Duuuuuuuuh

5. Never "borrow" from your retirement savings. Most of the time you'll incur stiff penalties for early withdrawals (gosh, that sounds sexy), and once you've started, it's a hard habit to break (at least until all your savings are gone).

Duh   Duuuh   Duuuuuuuuh

6. In order to avoid borrowing from your retirement savings for emergencies and other expenses, establish a separate emergency fund in a money market or savings account, ideally consisting of three to twelve months' worth of living expenses.

Duh   Duuuh   Duuuuuuuuh

7. Diversify your savings by investing in a range of stocks, bonds, CDs, and other types of instruments, rather than put all your eggs in one basket. A so-called asset allocation plan should help limit your risks and increase returns over the long run.

Duh   Duuuh   Duuuuuuuuh

8. Periodically rebalance your investments according to your asset allocation plan, as over time some portions of your portfolio will likely drift out of sync with the intended asset allocation (e.g., stocks may grow to be 60 percent of the total rather than, say, 50 percent, as called for in your asset allocation). If you don't rebalance, you defeat the whole purpose of having an asset allocation plan.

Duh   Duuuh   Duuuuuuuuh

9. Don't try to time the stock market (i.e., get in and out of the market to avoid losses and maximize gains); no one can do it successfully.

Duh   Duuuh   Duuuuuuuuh

10. Related to 9, it's better in the long run to buy and hold quality stocks than to buy and sell stocks constantly for potential short-term gains (aka day trading). Not only do you stand a better chance of building wealth over the long haul, but to buy and hold has significant tax advantages over day trading.

Duh   Duuuh   Duuuuuuuuh

11. Invest in stocks periodically, according to a regular schedule (e.g., monthly), rather than all at once. This allows you to maximize the principle of dollar cost averaging, mitigating the possibility of buying high.

Duh   Duuuh   Duuuuuuuuh

12. It's a mistake, financially and emotionally, to monitor your investments constantly. You'll drive yourself crazy and increase the risk of making rash decisions if you succumb to the temptation of incessantly checking the status of your investments online or in the newspaper. Barring some headline-making financial news, review the quarterly statements provided by your investment company for accuracy, and sit down once a year to really look at how things are going.

Duh   Duuuh   Duuuuuuuuh

10

Conclusion: Go Forth and Be Cheap

Not everything that can be counted counts, and not everything that counts can be counted. —Albert Einstein

Success is getting what you want. Happiness is wanting what you get. —Dale Carnegie

If you're looking for something more in life, you're likely to find it in something less. —the Ultimate Cheapskate

"Life's too short not to enjoy it!" a friend of mine once protested when I was espousing my views on the virtues of leading the cheapskate lifestyle.

His breaking point came that evening, when I asked for a doggy bag not only for my leftovers, but for everyone else's at our table in the five-star restaurant where he was holding court. And I thought I was on my best behavior; at least I wasn't pillaging adjacent tables.

"That's exactly what *I'm* saying," I responded. And we all laughed. Within a few years that friend, an ambitious, hard-driving, "gonna take some time for myself after this next deal is done" young man, died in an airplane crash—in his own plane; a personal jet he was piloting with several others on board.

That dinner was now more than twenty years ago, in the go-go 1980s, when the term "conspicuous consumer" became part

of our vernacular. It would be a disservice to my friend to reduce him to a caricature of Wall Street greed; he was a generous, kindhearted, caring man. Nonetheless, his North Star was
money, and the stuff he could proudly buy with it. When he
died, I thought long and hard about that and the good-natured
argument we'd had over dinner.

Consumed by Consumption

The term "conspicuous consumer," one who buys and owns
stuff at warp speed, primarily for the intrinsic pleasure of showing others that he's doing so, may just be a catchphrase developed by some creative journalist in the 1980s. Then again, he
or she had plenty of facts to work with:

- Per capita consumption in the United States rose
  approximately 45 percent between the 1970s and the
  1990s (*Seattle Times*).
- Percentage of college freshmen who reported thinking
  it's essential to be well off financially was 44 percent in
  1967, 76 percent in 1987.
- In 1981 between two-thirds and three-quarters of all
  housewares purchased were to replace a worn-out item.
  By 1987 fewer than half of all such purchases were as
  replacements (*Wall Street Journal*).
- Percentage of teenage girls in 1986 who reported
  store shopping as their favorite activity was 93
  percent.
- The banner year in which shopping centers in the
  United States (32,563) surpassed the number of high
  schools was 1987.

- Increase in consumer debt during the 1980s was 140 percent.

But it's also true that the trend toward turbocharged consumption started before the 1980s and continues to this day. The consumption curve may have steepened during the 1980s, but it still hasn't leveled off or started to decline. I think you know that's true, at least in your own life; otherwise you wouldn't be reading this book, let alone its final chapter.

Cheap: The Next Cool?

Live by the cool, die by the cool. Conspicuous consumers owe their existence to the fact that having money and stuff has come to mean they're cool. So I suppose the only way to counteract that is to show that being cheap is cooler.

It's time for the cheapskate to replace that worn-out old omni-consuming creature from the 1980s as the new cool kid in school. The cheapskate: someone who proudly consumes less and conserves more, because it increases the quality of his own life and the lives of everyone else on the planet, as well as the health of the planet itself.

That's the cornerstone of my Cheap Pride movement, of which you are now an honorary member. My dream is for people like me (and you, I suspect) to rise up from the back aisles of the Dollar Store and say, "Yes, we are cheap, but we are generous, kind, and happy because of it. We refuse to spend our time making money so that we can buy things we don't want or need, particularly when so many others have so very little. Our lives and our time are more precious than that. We are cheap, but we are proud . . . *and we are cool.*"

Our Cheap Pride Platform is simple but profound:

- We are too self-confident and too smart to let others convince us that more is always better and that we need things we don't.
- We live within our means always and live below our means if we can.
- We understand that we need enough—and we know exactly what *enough* is for us—and beyond that we need no more.
- We believe that waste is morally wrong and that excess is waste waiting to happen.
- We would rather learn to do things for ourselves than to rely on money to get others to do things for us.
- We consume things sparingly, thoughtfully, and fully; therefore things do not consume us.
- We take care of ourselves, our possessions, our planet, and others, rather than pay a higher price to repair benign neglect or do nothing as it occurs.
- We know, with absolute certainty, that you cannot chop a basketball in half with an ax, even on a five-dollar bet.

What Time Do You Have?

No, I don't mean what time does your watch say. I mean the question that's always hanging over each of us, contemplated or not, from the moment we're born. How much time do you have left here on this earth?

Very few people know the answer to that question with any certainty, and those who do—the terminally ill, inmates on death row, and other unfortunates—probably wish they didn't.

For the rest of us the only thing we know with certainty is that eventually there'll be an answer. If you think of life as a highway, as I've encouraged you to do in the preceding pages, it may have occurred to you that that answer could be just around the next bend in the road. Or not; you won't know until you get there.

But you do know that there are many intersections along the highway, many choices you must make, and many—too many—of those involve money and the trade-off between money and time. By being cheap, skipping the Money Steps, you're valuing time and the things you can do with it more than money and the things you can buy with it. You're determined to amass a quality of life and not just a quantity of stuff.

Congratulations. You've exited the Road to Riches and you're headed off down the Road to True Riches, the Highway to Happiness. Slow down and say hello when you pass me along the way. I'll be the tall guy on the bicycle.

AFTERWORD

Thanks for taking the time to read my book. I hope you liked it.

If you have any questions, suggestions, or ideas to share, I'd love to hear from you. You can contact me through my Web site, www.UltimateCheapskate.com.

Also, if your book club or other group is interested in discussing my book, please let me know. I'll drop by if I'm in the area or will gladly be part of your meeting by phone, if you'd like. I'll even use my own phone card to call you!

Stay cheap, and always remember: Live every day as if it were your last because one day you'll be right.

CHEAP-SPEAK GLOSSARY

From the Ultimate Cheapskate

BOGOF—A coupon or other discount offer that allows you to "buy one and get one free" (aka two for one or twofer). In hardened cheapskate circles, BOGOFing is the sport of producing your two-for-one coupon just as the other guy is paying full price for his, thereby getting your portion for free.

BOUTIQUE—French for "small shop with big prices," a perfect place for the insecure to dispose of their excess wealth.

BROKER—1. *n.* a professional trader or middleman dealing in stocks or some other special market or commodity. 2. *adj.* probable outcome of listening too closely to the *n.*

CARPE CRAPE!—Latin for "Seize the crap!," the rallying cry for curb shoppers worldwide.

CELLULITES—People who use their cell phones not for communications but simply to piss me off. Cellulites now constitute more than 98.2 percent of all cell phone users worldwide, according to my research.

CHEAPSKATE—Someone who proudly consumes less and conserves more, because it increases the quality of his or her own life and the lives of everyone else on the planet, as well as the health of the planet itself. A member of the Cheap Pride movement; the new cool kid on the block. (Antonym: CONSPICUOUS CONSUMER)

CHEAP PRIDE MOVEMENT—A voluntary, spontaneous movement of people like me who are finally rising up from the back aisles of the dollar store and saying, "Yes, we are cheap, but we are also generous, kind, and happy. We refuse to spend our whole lives making money we really don't need to make or spend in order to enjoy life!"

CHERRY-PICKING—The age-old cheapskate practice of buying only the best-of-the-best sales items at various grocery stores and other retailers.

CONTRA ECONOMICS—My theory that the vast majority of the American economy actually consists of corresponding transactions that effectively cancel each other out—for example, spending on unwanted hair removal (approximately $2 billion annually) and spending with the hope of promoting hair growth (approximately $2 billion annually). If you adjust for the effect of Contra Economics, I believe the actual size of the U.S. economy is slightly smaller than that of Lithuania.

COUPONEER—A cheapskate sect, normally dressed in stretch slacks. The scissor-wielding, glazed-eyed shoppers in the grocery stores who live for double-coupon days. (WARNING: Rarefied triple coupon days may cause Couponeers to faint by aisle 5.)

CURB SHOPPING—Picking up items (aka drive buys) set out along the street on trash collection day. An upscale alternative to Dumpster diving, particularly if you curb shop in exclusive neighborhoods; check with your local public services department for trash collection days in targeted neighborhoods. ANOTHER TIP: Target college towns the week students get out of school for the summer; they throw away *everything* (before they move back home with Mom and Dad, because they have nothing). Carpe crape!

CUSHION MINING—Stealthily searching for lost change in the furniture of hotel lobbies and other public venues. The preferred method is to sit casually on the furniture and inconspicuously slide your hands between the cushions. If apprehended, just say you think you lost your keys. Careful, though, you never know what you'll find down some cracks; my general rule is: "If it's sticky, don't pickie."

DEBTOR DEMENTIA–A semidelusional state commonly triggered by assuming a home mortgage or other large debt. It's the body's way of protecting that portion of the human brain that deals with rational thinking. Because of the size and scope of the transaction, the dollars involved seem like Monopoly money and the idea that you'll ever live to see the loan paid off seems like a fairy tale.

DESIGNATED CHEAPSKATE–A responsible individual appointed to discourage others from rampant spending during group shopping excursions. Designated cheapskates are advised to leave their own money and credit cards at home and to remind others in the group of recent purchases that they already regret or have forgotten about. If group members refuse to curb their spending, as a last resort the designated cheapskate should ask them how they're coming along on their retirement savings.

DILLY WHACKER–Coach Sacstretcher's term for the male reproductive organ. Derived from the Latin root (so to speak) *dillium whackeius*. Sacstretcher is now a successful personal financial advisor.

DILUTER–A cheapskate, in the tradition of my grandpa Yeager, who believes that the recommended dose / strength of all products is overstated by the manufacturer in order to increase consumption. As a result, diluters add water and other less expensive substances to stretch supplies of things like milk, juice, and detergent.

DOLLAR MAXIMUM ZONE OR DMZ–The Ultimate Cheapskate's rule of thumb when shopping for foodstuff. If it costs more than a dollar per pound, think long and hard before putting it in your shopping cart.

ECONOMIC ENEMA–The tough love alternative for those spendthrifts incapable of a self-imposed fiscal fast. Because of its graphic nature, this subject will be described in greater detail in a later book.

ENOUGHASAURUS—The beast within each of us, he / she that must be satisfied. Slaying or at least satisfying your *Enoughasaurus* is a matter of deciding what's enough for you and then designing your priorities and life around it.

FANCIFUL FINANCIER'S SYNDROME—The tendency to overmanage your investments, making frequent, precipitous changes based on your belief that you're smarter than you really are.

FISCAL FAST—A therapeutic exercise in self-discipline in which you force yourself to go for an extended period of time (ideally a week or more) without spending *any* money.

FOOD COST PYRAMID—An upside-down pyramid, overlaid on the USDA Food Pyramid, that proves that the best food for you also happens to cost the least. Hallelujah! If there is an intelligent designer, she's a cheapskate.

GPS HOMES—Monster houses of five thousand plus square feet that require a Global Positioning System to locate all the rooms; the native habitat of the house climber.

HIERARCHY OF MOOLAH MANAGEMENT—The priorities for managing your personal finances to ensure maximum life satisfaction, per the Ultimate Cheapskate. Contrary to the advice of many personal finance pundits, maximizing the growth of your investment portfolio is the lowest priority in the hierarchy, with the top priority being—surprise, surprise—reducing your dependency on money by SPENDING LESS.

HOBBY PORN—How-to books that inspire do-it-yourselfers through the use of full-color photos more than words.

HOUSE CLIMBERS—People who continually trade up to increasingly larger, more expensive homes in the belief that it will make them rich. I doubt that it will, and I'm quite certain it won't make them happy.

INNER MISER—The voice of financial reason and good judgment that lives within each of us. Your inner miser knows that buying that new pair of shoes won't make you any happier, but most people refuse to embrace the sage advice of their inner misers.

LIFE-CRAFTS–The best of all possible hobbies, ones that you not only enjoy but that save you big bucks in the long run—things like cooking, gardening, and home repair.

MAD CAP FUNDS–A small amount of funds (maybe 5 percent) set aside in your total portfolio for you to invest in individual stocks of your own choosing. With luck the return will be decent, but regardless, it will help to keep you interested, involved, and away from making precipitous decisions about the other 95 percent of your investments.

MANDATORY WAITING PERIOD–Your own personal Brady bill. When it comes to discretionary spending, wait at least one full week between the time you first see an item in a store and the time you go back to buy it.

MATH CONFUSION–Mass confusion regarding issues of simple mathematics. As with mass confusion, a mob mentality triggers irrational thinking and behavior. For example, "I can't pay off my mortgage or I'll lose my tax deduction!"

MILLION-DOLLAR MANTRA–The oft-repeated advice offered by financial planners regarding how much money you need to retire: "You need at least a million dollars to retire—and maybe more!" I'd have more confidence in this prognostication if the financial advisors I've spoken with actually understood more about my individual financial situation than I do, and that's not a very high bar. (In fact, it's a swim-up bar.)

MISER ADVISERS–Founding members of my Cheap Pride movement who agree to share their ideas and observations about spending less and enjoying life more. Candidates for Miser Adviser status must complete the following Declaration of Indespend-ence: "I'm so cheap that I _____." To register as a Miser Adviser, visit www.UltimateCheapskate.com.

MONEY STEP—The default setting for most people today. The assumption that we must:

> Earning money
>> To spend money
>>> To get what you want
[. . . or at least what you think you want]

This book shows that that's rarely, if ever, the case.

MONEY STEP AEROBICS—Cheapskate exercise, like mowing your lawn and walking to work; exercise that trims not only your waistline but also your spending.

ORMAN-GASM—A climax of sexual excitement caused by analyzing or discussing one's financial portfolio (Ref. Suzie Orman).

PERMANENT STANDARD OF LIVING—By deciding early in life what's enough for you to live on (SEE *Enoughasaurus*, SLAYING OF) and never exceeding it, even as your earnings rise, you'll be able to enjoy life more while spending less.

RE-CANTING—Transferring inexpensive spirits and box wine into premium brand-name bottles in order to impress your unsuspecting snob friends. (Antonym: DECANTING)

RENAISSANCE MISER—A cheapskate with well-rounded interests and hobbies that are both enjoyable and cost-effective. By consciously shaping your interests and passions in life, you'll enjoy life more and spend less.

RETURN MAILING—An unethical and probably illegal practice employed by unscrupulous skinflints, but never by the Ultimate Cheapskate. By using a self-addressed *un*stamped envelope (with your name indicated as the addressee and the true recipient's name and address as the return address), the post office will "return" the letter to the intended recipient marked "Insufficient Postage."

RETURN ON NONINVESTMENT (RONI)–The total, true net effect of choosing not to spend money on something. (Antonym: RETURN ON INVESTMENT, or ROI.)

REVERSE FOCUS GROUP–An exercise designed to allow you to rate your vulnerability to the approximately three thousand advertisements you're exposed to every day and to improve your defense mechanisms.

SELFISHLY EMPLOYED–Being able to pursue your interests and passions as employment without undue concern over income.

SPENDING PROCRASTINATION–When it comes to discretionary spending, putting off until tomorrow what you could buy today is a virtue, not a vice. (See *MANDATORY WAITING PERIOD*)

TAKING A BYE–A spending strategy, particularly effective in the case of technology spending, whereby you consciously forgo purchasing one or more "next generations" of new technology / products with no net loss of productivity, profitability, or other hardships.

"WHAT THE HELL WAS I THINKING?" AUDIT: An annual accounting exercise involving butcher paper, a card table, and a bingo dauber that allows you to learn from your past spending mistakes and get your financial house in order.

HIGHLY RECOMMENDED PIT STOPS
ALONG THE ROAD TO TRUE RICHES

This book is crammed full of additional resources and contacts to help you along the Road to True Riches, but there are a few venerable ones that deserve special attention:

Center for a New American Dream (www.NewDream.org)

This nonprofit membership organization helps Americans "consume responsibly to protect the environment, enhance quality of life, and promote social justice." From fighting the battle against junk mail, to promoting Carbon Conscious Consumerism, to tips for simplifying the holidays, this group deserves your attention— and your support as a member or donor.

Consumer Reports (www.ConsumerReports.org)

I know: Your great aunt won't buy a bra without consulting Consumer Reports first. But—that disturbing visual aside—they really are worth their weight in spandex. Everyone talks about "*best buys*," but only the nonprofit outfit Consumer Reports does the science. Read their reports online, through a subscription, or at the library, just so long as you read them before making major purchases.

New Road Map Foundation (www.newroadmap.org)

This is the nonprofit educational foundation that grew out of the benchmark book *Your Money or Your Life* by Joe Dominquez and Vicki Robin (Penguin, 1999). The foundation offers a variety of programs and other tools for promoting personal financial freedom as a path to community service and social well-being. See also www.yourmoneyoryourlife.org.

The Tightwad Gazette

When Amy Dacyczyn published the last issue of her acclaimed *Tightwad Gazette* newsletter in 1996, she felt that she'd said everything that could be said regarding tips for frugal living. And more than a decade later, I agree: She's still said it all. Nearly seven years' worth of the newsletter have been compiled in *The Complete Tightwad Gazette* (Villard, 1998), which is the bible of practical daily tips for spending less.

www.UltimateCheapskate.com

Let's keep in touch through my Web site, where I post my latest advice for how to *enjoy life more by spending less*. Sign up as a Miser Adviser (free, of course) and you can win free stuff and receive my weekly Cheap Talk blog. Stay Cheap!

About the author

JEFF YEAGER has run nonprofit agencies and is now a writer and the creator of the Web site www.ultimatecheapskate.com. He has appeared on *Today* several times. He lives happily and frugally in Accokeek, Maryland, with his wife, Denise.